WHAT
YOU NEED
IS
WHAT
YOU'VE GOT

WHAT YOU NEED IS WHAT YOU'VE GOT

Rediscovering, Developing and Using Your Inner Resources

Larry & Valere Althouse

SAMUEL WEISER, INC.
York Beach, Maine

First published in 1989 by
Samuel Weiser, Inc.
Box 612
York Beach, Maine 03910

Library of Congress Cataloging-in-Publication Data

Althouse, Larry.
    What you need. . .is what you've got/by Larry & Valere
Althouse.
        p.   cm.
    Bibliography: p.
    ISBN 0-87728-691-4
    1. Autonomy (Psychology)   2. Self-reliance.
3. Self-control.   4. Self-realization.   I. Althouse, Valere.
II. Title.
BF575.A88A46 1989   88-13100
158′.1--dc19   CIP

Typeset in 11 point Baskerville
Printed in the United States of America
by Edwards Brothers, Inc.

To

Roswitha

Because she had the place,
We found the time.

TABLE OF CONTENTS

ACKNOWLEDGMENTS

Over the years we have learned so much from so many people that it is virtually impossible to acknowledge everyone to whom we are indebted. We have been privileged to study in person with many excellent teachers and with others through their books, articles and tapes. Complimenting our own experiences, many of these ideas and concepts have become second nature to us and we are not always aware of from whom we first received them. Some of our indebtedness is indicated in the "Resources" section of each chapter. Most of the material in this book has been presented as workshops for the participants in our semi-annual Spa Holiday programs in Badgastein, Austria. We are grateful to these people for their many helpful comments and suggestions. Should you be interested in joining one of these Spa Holiday programs, more information may be obtained from Friendship Tours, 4412 Shenandoah Avenue, Dallas, Texas, 75205.

We owe a special word of thanks to the Watsons, Bakkens and Biersteins who repeatedly urged that we "get all that stuff in a book," and to our friends in Badgastein, Austria, who helped us in so many ways and looked after our needs during the writing of this manuscript: Angelika and Erika Gugganig, Walter and Marianne Kofler, Dr. Hans Woratschka, Roswitha Franzmair, and the whole staff at the Hotel Elizabethpark.

INTRODUCTION

What would be more exciting and dramatic than to begin this book by saying: *Read this and never take another pill to stay awake, go to sleep, ease pain, heal sickness, manage stress, deal with tension, pep you up, or calm you down.* Our purpose, however, is not to guarantee you freedom from all external resources. Rather it is to convince you that within *you* are all the resources you need to meet the demands of daily life. More than you might ever dream!

Of course there are times when you need help from something or someone outside yourself—a physician, priest, machine—yes, perhaps even a pill—but we believe that you can discover, as we have, that, for the most part, WHAT YOU NEED IS WHAT YOU'VE GOT WITHIN YOU!

It may be that you already know that—at least intellectually. But from what we have observed, it seems that you might habitually reach for something outside yourself when you are challenged, and almost never turn to your own inner potential as a matter of first resort. This seductive attitude—always looking for the answers somewhere outside yourself—is responsible for the insecurity we see today. Is it any wonder that the younger generation (and some not so young), after several decades of being bombarded with mass media advertising that promises relief from just about anything through the simple act of swallowing a pill, looks for the "highs" and "cools" of life in hard drugs? Take a look at your daily newspaper. Is there not an overwhelming suggestion that happiness, success, and contentment can be purchased exclusively through an installment plan, credit card, or an 800-number?

Almost every major religion of the world has, in some way or another, taught that the greatest resources in life are those which we find in our own God-given humanity. Although Christian theologians may argue over just what Jesus meant when he said, "The kingdom of heaven is within you," (Luke 12:21 King James Version), it is hard to read the four Gospels of the New Testament without concluding that Christ taught people essentially to look within themselves for both the source of the problem and the resources with which to meet it.

Today, impressive verification is being found to substantiate this conviction concerning inner human potential. People with migraine and tension headaches are discovering that they can either eliminate or control these conditions through the use of biofeedback training by learning how to enlist their own inner defense mechanisms to avoid or diminish pain. At the same time, Dr. Herbert Benson of Harvard Medical School and Beth Israel Hospital tells of helping people to learn to control their hypertension (high blood pressure) through a simple method of meditation and without the use of either medications or machines.[1] Other researchers have discovered that controlable personality factors play a vital role in the incidence and healing of many serious illnesses.

With all due respect to those who say that the future of humanity is to be found in the exploration of outer space, there is a growing consensus all over the world—spanning a great variety of disciplines, ideologies, and cultures—that the ultimate frontier will be explored and crossed in inner space. We are convinced that the universe within is of more consequence than the one "out there."

---

[1]Herbert Benson, M.D., with Miriam Z. Klipper, *The Relaxation Response* (New York: William Morrow, 1975).

Without getting further involved in these and other arguments, we can unequivocally promise you that the exploration of the concepts and techniques in this book can help you much more successfully and satisfyingly meet the demands of daily life. Whether you ever again take another pill, see another doctor, or rely on another machine is not our concern. We want you to learn to use what is within you.

This book is based upon two presuppositions: we believe that most of the answers of life are to be found within, and we are committed to the proposition that, by taking charge of your life, you can use your inner resources to make your life more fulfilling. This means you will have to give up the self-limiting perception of yourself as a victim. In our counseling, we have found that many people are obsessed with the idea that they are victims — of bad breaks, unhappy situations, poor health, failure, inadequate parentage, insufficient family means, too much affluence, bad geography, unfavorable constellations, congenital weaknesses, exploitation, and so on. Many people struggle through life with the conviction that some Thing or some One is in control of their lives and directing them toward a destiny they did not choose for themselves.

In Christianity this takes the form of "predestination" — the belief that everything has been preordained. In Eastern religious thought it may be expressed as a fatalistic "karma." For other people it is a simple belief in "fate" or "kismet," while for others it is nothing more than resignation: "That's just the way I am!" Today, this insidious suspicion has been undergirded by some of the concepts of behavioristic psychology — the idea that we are essentially victims of conditioning.

Fortunately, mounting evidence in many fields leads us to challenge this deterministic view of life. Dr. Hans Selye and other researchers in the field of stress tell us that it is not experience that causes stress or, more accurately, distress, but the way in which you react to those stressors. Drs. Elmer and Alyce Green of the Menninger Clinic have demonstrated repeatedly that you have power to assert conscious control over the functions of your body that are normally autonomic or unconsciously directed. In addition, one of the primary tenets of the holistic health movement is that you can take responsibility for (and charge of) your own body.

In the fall of 1982, we heard Nobel Laureate scientist Sir John Eccles tell the Isthmus Institute of Dallas, Texas that he was convinced he had discovered how nerves use chemical transmitters to send messages to the brain. In other words, he was asserting that the mind is separate from the brain and, more important still, is in control of the brain. This helps to verify the concept of free will and moral responsibility. At one point, he told the Isthmus Institute audience, "I want to insist that we do have this moral responsibility stemming from free will, of the ability of the mind to work on the brain." Responding favorably to Eccles' assertion, United Methodist theologian Albert Outler commented, "Thus, our thoughts affect our actions and our lives are not at the blind mercies of Chance and Necessity, the two oldest gods in the human pantheon."[2]

Dr. William James, the father of American psychology, once declared that, "The greatest discovery of our generation is that human beings, by changing their inner attitudes, can change the outer aspects of their lives."[3] Since the mind, or psyche, has been demonstrated to have so much influence over your brain and body — including your undiscovered and undeveloped potential — it follows that, by changing your thoughts, attitudes, and perceptions, you can change your life — and, very often, your world.

Some people prefer to think of themselves as in the inexorable grip of something quite beyond their control. But you were not created to be a victim. You were created to be a victor.

---

[2]Quotations from Sir John Eccles and Albert Outler are from our own notes from Eccles' January 29, 1983, address to the Isthmus Institute in Dallas, Texas.

[3]As quoted by Dr. Elmer Green of the Menninger Clinic, Topeka, Kansas, in his address to the Isthmus Institute, December 6, 1984.

As the Apostle Paul puts it to the church in Galatia: *For freedom Christ has set us free; stand fast therefore and do not submit again to a yoke of slavery* (Galatians 5:1). Not even to an unconsciously self-imposed yoke of slavery that is forged deep within the depths of your own psyche.

If you are willing to take a look deep within yourself and assume responsibility for—and control over—what you find there, turn the page and begin your quest of humanity's ultimate frontier.

CHAPTER

KICK
THE
WORRY HABIT

Larry used to be a worrier. He worried before something happened; he worried while it was happening; he worried after it had happened; and he worried if it didn't happen! In a sense, he covered all the bases with worry. When admonished not to worry so much, he would usually respond, "I can't help it; that's just the way I am."

One day while making a pastoral call in the hospital, he stood and looked in the large window of the maternity floor nursery. There was row upon row of newborn infants. Some were sleeping; a few were crying; one or two were entertaining what later would be regarded as smiles. But not one of them, he observed, wrinkled a brow in worry. "That," he mused under his breath, "is something they'll learn in time."

As he walked down the hall, the implications of what he had just said to himself hit him like the proverbial ton of bricks. People learn to worry; no one is born a worrier! "Not even me!"

he said aloud, earning him a raised eyebrow from a passing nurse.

The more he thought about it in the days, weeks, and months that followed that moment of revelation, the more certain he became of the following conclusions:

1) Worry was something he had learned to do — and do well!

2) It had become a habit, an automatic response which was a way of life.

3) If he had learned *how* to do it, he could also learn how *not* to do it. If it was a habit, he could form a new habit.

But why had he learned to worry? That question kept puzzling him. He finally realized that he learned worry from other people. He simply emulated the behavior of people around him. Growing up through the Great Depression of the 1930s, he had seen a lot of worry on the faces around him. Although they had tried not to communicate their anxieties to him, his parents had found a great deal over which to worry during those years.

Not only was worry a norm for those times, it was also characteristic of his particular culture. The Pennsylvania Dutch, hardened by adversities and uncertainties even before they migrated to America from Germany, took a kind of self-protective outlook on life. Expecting the worst was a kind of talisman against whatever life might bring. If you expected the worst, you were not likely to be surprised when it or something less threatening came along. In fact, if life was not as hard as you expected it to be, it was like a bonus! A gift! So, living under the constant expectation of hearing the "other shoe drop" became a way of life, a way of coping with life's uncertainties. He remembered his grandmother's funny little laugh whenever she received bad news. It was as if she was greeting the devil with: "See, you didn't surprise us; we were expecting you!"

He also realized that even though these cultural and environmental influences might have gotten him off in the wrong direction in meeting life's uncertainties, they were by no means the reason for his continuance of the stupid habit. Not all his Pennsylvania Dutch peers of the Great Depression were habitually negative toward life. Some, in fact, didn't seem to worry much at all, even when he was convinced they should. So, there had to be some other reason or reasons.

In time he came to realize that much of the worry habit was related to a tendency to overdramatize the challenges of daily living. Once again, some of this was probably learned from his mileu, but it also must have served his own personal purposes, too, to have become so habitual. What purposes?

An oversensitive child (which we realize is still another question rather than an answer), he probably found the habit of worry an unconscious defense mechanism against disappointment. Also, overdramatization was possibly a means of getting attention or focussing it upon himself—this, despite the fact that his parents gave him lots of unsolicited attention.

In retrospect, it seems that his worry habit manifested in a number of ways. He learned to feel more intensely about situations than was warranted. Subtleties of emotion were not enough: if he was going to be afraid of something, a lot of fear was better than a little bit. Thus, in saying "he learned to feel more intensely," we are indicating that he unconsciously taught his mind to misperceive events and his endocrine system to oversecrete in responding to these misperceptions.

Certain outward physiological responses became habits—a wrinkled brow—how else would people know he was worrying?—a tightening of muscles in the neck and shoulders, a slight clenching of the teeth—he tried to learn to do it the way his father did, but never was successful—and a host of "nervous reactions" with his hands and fingers. (These are habits he is still trying to unlearn, sometimes successfully, sometimes not.)

He adopted an exaggerated mode of thought and speech to match his misperceptions: minor inconveniences were "terrible," modest setbacks became "disasters," slight pain "killed" him, fifteen minutes of exasperation "ruined a whole day," and an anticipated outcome of a bad situation was often, "I'll just die!"

Are you addicted to linguistic overkill? Exaggerated language might even be the rule rather than the exception in our day. But just because it is so popularly employed doesn't mean for one minute that it doesn't have harmful effects. Language helps to shape your perceptions because the unconscious mind doesn't seem to have the capacity to distinguish between the literal and figurative language you use.

In psychosomatic studies, for example, it has often been found that, when you repeatedly say, "He gives me a pain!" the unconscious may respond by making those words a self-fulfilling prophecy. In stress research it has similarly been discovered that it is only when you perceive a stressor-experience as "disastrous," that it has the power to overtax your body with stress.

Larry also came to realize that worry could be a substitute for action. Fearful that he would make the wrong action response to a challenge, he delayed making that choice by continuing to deliberate among the possibilities long after the deliberation ceased being constructive. Actually, that is the key difference between worry and legitimate fear and anxiety. These are often logical responses to the experiences of life. But they need not become permanent conditions or long lasting ones. Once they alert you to a problem and its severity, and motivate you to respond to the challenge, they serve no continuing purpose. In fact, they may well become counter-productive. That is really what worry is, a counter-productive preoccupation of the mind and body with a problem or challenge. If your fear or anxiety is causing you to work toward a solution or at least a response, then it's probably not worry.

Someone said that "worry is like a rocking chair: it gives you something to do, but it doesn't get you anywhere." That's right! Worry is not thinking that gets you somewhere, but thinking that gets you nowhere. It is unnecessary, unproductive, and even self-defeating. It doesn't solve your problem, it keeps you from solving it. Sometimes there is not too much you can do to respond to a situation, and worrying keeps you from even doing the little you could do.

We have often puzzled over why people are so reluctant to give up the habit of worry, even when they are convinced of its uselessness and harmful effects. Larry had experienced some of this reluctance himself. It seemed almost that in some strange, perverse way he "liked" worrying. It gave him something "exciting" to do. Some of the challenges of life, when perceived realistically, are actually pretty boring, and worrying tends to "juice them up" a bit.

Thus, he has sometimes suggested to counselees that perhaps they, too, had come to "enjoy" their worrying in the same way that some people seem to "enjoy poor health." The usual response to this suggestion ranges from grudging tolerance to the possibility to downright vigorous denial. Yet, how else to explain our strange attachment to this destructive habit?

Several years ago *Time* magazine carried a feature article on stress, its causes, its effects, and its management. Dr. Paul Rosch, Director of the American Institute of Stress in Yonkers, New York, was quoted as saying: "People today have become addicted to their own adrenaline secretions."[1] We knew he was referring to the fact that different emotions trigger the secretion of different biochemical solutions in the body. Fear results in the secretion of the powerful hormone, adrenaline, while anger causes the secretion of noradrenaline (sounding similar, but actually quite different). Thus, we understood Dr. Rosch to be indicating that many people allow their bodies to become accustomed to excessive — often destructive — amounts of hormones. Perhaps people "like" to worry because they have become habitually accustomed to excessive amounts of hor-

---

[1] From "Stress: Can We Cope?" *Time,* June 6, 1983, p. 49.

mones in their biochemical systems. Overexcitement (from purposeful misperception) is "desirable" because it is sensed as "necessary" in the same way that a cigarette or glass of vodka may seem to be "necessary" to the addict.

Surprisingly, some people still want to know, "What's wrong with worrying?" Actually, you don't have to be a mental giant to determine what's wrong with this habit. For one thing, because it *is* a habit, it is automatic (or unconsciously conditioned) behavior. It robs you of your opportunity to be in charge of your own life. It shapes your life for you without recourse to the best resources of intelligence and judgment that are available.

Stress research has conclusively proven what most people have long known: worry saps your strength — your vitality you need to meet the challenges of life. Often it is far more exhausting than the action for which it has become the substitute. It takes from you, never adds to you.

We have already indicated that worry distorts perception. It is both a cause and result of distorted perception. Worrying magnifies problems and dangers while minimizing or obliterating your resources. The more you worry, the more distorted your perceptions.

When you're confronted with a problem or a challenge in your daily life, one of the most necessary resources to assist you is the power of concentration. The ability to focus your full power upon a situation plays a big role in determining the success or failure of your response. For example, in football, a potential forward pass receiver needs his full concentration to catch and hold the ball thrown to him. If he gives some of his concentration to the thought that someone may tackle him just as he receives the ball, it may be enough of a diversion to cause him to mishandle and drop the ball. Worry causes you to "drop" lots of "balls" you should have been able to "catch."

Furthermore, worry paralyzes your will. We have already indicated that worry can become a substitute for purposeful action. The more you worry, the less you seem able to act. Part of the seductiveness of worry is the false assumption that, when you are worrying, you are doing something. Well, you are, but what you are doing is not constructive — and that's the only kind of doing that matters.

There seems to be increasing evidence that worry, particularly habitual worry, may either lead to or, in reality, be depression. Sometimes called "the common cold of emotional health," depression is an abnormal (meaning: not the way you were intended to be) condition which afflicts "some of the people all of the time, and all of the people some of the time," bringing misery, anguish and defeat to all who allow it to take up permanent, even if seasonal, residence within.

A few years ago we came across a book which confirmed what we ourselves had seemed to experience both personally and professionally for many years. According to Dr. David Burns of the University of Pennsylvania, research and clinical experience indicates that, contrary to what may be popularly believed, depression is the result — not the cause — of negative perceptions. You do not first "feel" depressed and then think negatively, says Burns. You think negatively and these thoughts cause you to "feel" depressed. Your body chemistry is determined by your cognition (perception and your thoughts about those perceptions), and when you're depressed, according to Burns, your cognition is distorted and faulty in much the same way as the cognition of people with serious mental illnesses.

People become depressed, not because their thinking is too "realistic," but because it isn't realistic enough. It is the result of seeing challenges in a distorted perspective. It is sick or defective reasoning. Every bout of depression is preceded and triggered, says Burns, by a distorted cognition.

What this means for sufferers of depression — occasional or chronic — is that you can rid yourselves of depression, because you can rid yourself of the distorted thoughts that give rise to it. No pill, no machine, no surgery can do that for you, but you can do it for yourself — if you want to.

We wouldn't suggest for one moment, however, that because the choice is yours, that you are all you have. While it is true that you are in charge of yourself, it is also important to realize that, for the most part, you are not in charge of others. Part of learning to assume autonomy over yourself is to learn the limits of your autonomy. One of the reasons that people worry is because they are stuck with the distorted perception that they should be able to control everything. But life teaches you that there are lots of things beyond your control.

For Larry, learning not to worry meant accepting the fact that he was not God. Like many clergymen, Larry had a lot of godly expectations for himself. He believed that if he worked hard enough, thought clearly enough, and persisted long enough, there was no problem he couldn't solve. But then he came up against some problems that no amount of clear thought or hard work could solve, no matter how persistently he pursued them. In defeat, he finally discovered who he was — a mortal, finite human being. Human beings make mistakes, have limitations, and are not inexhaustible. In other words, leave some things to God, the cosmos, or whatever else it is you believe in.

Although he had long known the famous prayer of his former seminary professor, Dr. Reinhold Niebuhr, for the first time he began to understand what it means (not that it is at all obscure):

> O God, give us
> >serenity to accept what cannot be changed,
> courage to change what should be changed,
> And wisdom
> >to distinguish the one from the other.

Courage is not enough. Life also requires patience to wait for God, society, eternity, or whatever, to do what lies beyond you. And, most important of all, it requires that you know the difference — between the human and the divine, between God and yourself, between creature and Creator, between what is in your hands and what is not.

It may be a well-worn cliché, but Larry found that nothing could be more essential to him than to "Let go and let God." In a sense he had to learn to let go of a world that he never really had in his hands or on his shoulders. But so long as he thought he did, there was nothing to do but worry.

Larry has "kicked the worry habit." Actually, he found it wasn't really as much fun as it had seemed. There was no loss in giving it up, only gain. And you can experience that same "gain" for yourself.

HOW CAN YOU KICK THE WORRY HABIT?

When gripped by worry or depression, you can search for the distorted perspectives and ideas that give rise to them. For example, you might find you are worrying because of a perception that, "If he finds out that I did that, he'll never forgive me." Is that perception really true? Will "he" really "never forgive you," or will he just be angry with you for a while? There's a big difference between the two. Is there some other way you can change the perception? For example, if you go to him and tell him what you've done and why, might not the consequences be considerably less than if he simply "finds out"? (See *Feeling Good* by David Burns under the Resources listing for additional help with this method.)

It's easier to learn to limit worry than to avoid it altogether—at least in the beginning. Most worrying proceeds in a cyclical manner: the problem—your conclusions about it—what you think the result will be—expected fall-out—back to the problem, and so on. One of the reasons that worry is counter-productive is because it does not move from problem to solution, but from problem to possible solutions, back to problem. Like the rocking chair, it doesn't get you anywhere.

So, decide to limit yourself to no more than two statements of the problem and consequences. When you find that you have returned to the problem once again, arbitrarily shut off debate and move on to what you will do about it. Do not allow yourself to go back again and again.

Another way of approaching this is to decide on a time limit that you will allow yourself to devote to worry. Get yourself a timer, set it for one minute, and when the alarm sounds, make yourself move on to doing something about it. One minute is more than enough for something as useless as worry!

Make a conscious effort to change your overkill vocabulary. Whenever you find yourself describing to yourself or others a situation, problem, or challenge, check for overkill terms. For example, is your car really a "lemon," or are the expenditures you're having to make on it pretty much "par for the course?" Is that pain really "excruciating"—a reference to death on a cross—or is it more accurately very uncomfortable? Does she really "hate" you, or does she simply get annoyed with some of your habits? Is your boss really "a bastard" or does he simply have a greater sense of devotion to profit and loss than you do?

Occupy your mind with something positive, particularly when you find your worry returning repeatedly to haunt you. A negative cannot be cast out with another negative. It can only be pushed out of your consciousness by something positive. If someone says to you right now, "I don't want you to think about a hot fudge sundae," you are not very likely to do what you are told. But, if instead someone says, "Please visualize a thick, juicy steak," the hot fudge sundae will probably disappear from your attention. Therefore, to get rid of a thought or image that is dragging you down with worry, you need to use an equally or even more powerful thought or image to replace it. Telling yourself "I *won't* do that" only reinforces the power of the thing you want to get rid of. Instead, say "I *will* do this."

Several decades ago when Larry was a minister on the staff of a church in suburban New York City, he called on a new member of the congregation, who, he discovered, was confined to a wheelchair with a crippling, degenerative disease. Like many of us, he immediately responded by feeling sorry for her, only to discover that she didn't seem to feel sorry for herself. Instead of wondering why more people weren't doing things for her, she spent her days on the telephone and at the writing desk encouraging others, many of whom were physically much better off than she. She didn't have the opportunity to worry about the increasing ravages of her disease because her mind was too occupied doing things for other people.

Take an inventory of your worries. On a sheet of paper, draw four columns. Head the first column: "What I Worry About." Then list your favorite worries number one to infinity, if you have that many. Go back and put the headings on the other three columns: "Things I Can Change," "Things I Cannot Change," and "What Do I Need Here?"

Go back and review each of the worries on your list. With each, decide if it is something you can or cannot change and record that decision in the proper column. After having decided if your worry is something to be changed or not, think about what you need to do in order to live with that reality. For example: your husband is incurably ill, so what you may decide you need is patience, faith, or compassion—but not worry!

RESOURCES FOR FURTHER STUDY AND SELF-DEVELOPMENT

Burns, David D., M.D. *Feeling Good: The New Mood Therapy.* New York: Signet, 1983: Particularly Part I.

Dyer, Dr. Wayne W. *Your Erroneous Zones.* New York: Avon, 1977: Particularly Chapter V, "The Useless Emotions—Guilt And Worry."

Hoke, James H. *I Would If I Could and I Can*. New York: Berkley, 1982: Particularly Chapters 1, 2, and 3.

Hutschnecker, Arnold, M.D. *The Will to Live*. New York: Cornerstone, 1972. Part 1, "To Live Or Not To Live."

Weinberg, Dr. George. *Self Creation*. New York: Avon, 1979, Chapters 1–7.

CHAPTER

ACCENTUATE
THE
POSITIVE!

Look carefully at the glass depicted in figure 1 on page 14. Ordinarily, how would you describe it? Half full? Half empty?

Actually, it's both, isn't it? These are simply two different perspectives on the same reality. Actually, you can make airtight cases for both half-fullness and half-emptiness. Neither perspective is necessarily wrong, nor is either fully correct. To be quite accurate, you would have to say that the cup is half-full and half-empty.

Your visual equipment forces you to choose one perspective over the other, even though reason says both statements are true. The practical demands of daily life force you to operate on the basis of perspectives which you know are not fully and completely the truth. For example, you know intellectually that the apparently "solid" world that surrounds you is not really "solid." Everything, including this book and the chair you're sitting in, is a whirling mass of energy, the "solid" material of which is actually a small fraction of the "solid" image

Figure 1. Half full? Or half empty?

your mind perceives. If you saw this world as it really is, if you could hear all the sounds of the world around you instead of the limited audio range that protects you from sound "overload," you couldn't function.

Think about it: there is purpose behind the limiting of your perceptions. You know that things you cannot see — atoms, molecules, cosmic rays — are no less real because you cannot see them. Radio waves and sounds beyond the capability of your hearing are likewise no less real because you can't hear them. Because your mind is finite and because you can handle only so much sensory input, you cope by focusing your mind upon the essentials of daily living. So, even though you consciously or unconsciously exclude what you cannot see, hear, taste, touch or smell, you know full well that there is more than what your senses reveal. (How much more? That question would move us into philosophical and theological inquiries that are not within the scope of this chapter.) So, your experience is largely shaped by the perspectives upon which you choose to focus your attention. For the most part, you see what you choose to see.

For example, as we sit here writing this book, we are looking at a beautiful alpine vista before us — tall, straight evergreens, snow-capped peaks, golden sun, and a magnificent blue sky. If we were to willfully shift our perspective, however, we could see other things that for our present purposes we choose to exclude — the bubbles in the green paint on the railing bordering our balcony, a black beetle crawling along the ledge just beyond the railing, tiny airborne seeds floating through the air just a few feet beyond us, and, if we were to supplement the power of our own eyes with more sensitive and highly-focused equipment, we could also detect bacteria in the air, ultraviolet rays, dust particles, electrical waves, and the airplane that is producing the vapor trail we see arching across the sky.

Really, all of life is like that — a conscious or unconscious selection of the perspectives with which you will view your world and act upon it. You know there is more than your perspective, but you also know you have to limit your perspective and focus your attention and energies. When your choice of perspective is unconscious, it is essentially a habit. Normally, you don't think about which perspective you're going to use. For example, when Larry and I walked through the door onto our balcony, we did not deliberate either within ourselves or with each other as to what we were going to see. By habit, prior conditioning, we "lifted our eyes unto the hills" and saw what we expected to see. But, if for some reason we realized that there was something else on our balcony we needed to see — like the display screen on this typewriter — then we could and did consciously choose a different perspective to meet the needs of our chosen goals.

Many, many people we have counseled go through life experiencing it as essentially sad, painful, and evil because they see it through a very negative perspective. In justifying this perspective they say, "But that's the way the world is: just look around you, read of life's tragedies and injustices in the daily newspaper, view the rottenness and corruption on your television screen; what do you want us to do — make believe it's not there?"

No, we are not suggesting that you make believe that there are no negative realities in this world. What we are asking, however, is for you to acknowledge that, as with every perspective, every worldview, there is more than you can see.

And furthermore, we are asking you to realize that what you are seeing in the world is a limited, selective view. Yes, newspapers and television are full of depressing news, but this is a careful selection of negative data that is based on a conviction that people want to read and hear and see this. If, instead of telling you about one public officer in your community who has taken a bribe, the news focused on the 3,895 public servants who did not, you wouldn't give the news your attention. If, instead of telling you about three acts of violent crime in your metropolitan area, the media reported 384 charitable, benevolent and worthy deeds, you wouldn't buy the paper, read the magazine, or tune in the station.

The fact is, most of us seem to find negative news interesting and positive news dull, or to put it in terms of the marketplace — sin sells, virtue doesn't. So, in varying degrees, people tend to tune in to the negative or focus on it. But that doesn't mean that's all there is. That doesn't mean there is not lots of positive, constructive and uplifting activity in the world. It means simply that most people have consciously or unconsciously chosen to focus upon the negative, the destructive, and ultimately the life-defeating. So by habit we are accustomed to seeing the cup half-empty. And what you see is what you get.

It's ironic that people not only find the negative more interesting, but also tend to regard it as more real. If you read of charges of rape in the newspaper, you regard that as reality. If you read of a prisoner's protestations of innocence, you scoff at these as fabrications. Or, if as happened recently, the victim later recants her story and exonerates the prisoner, most people find it hard to accept the possibility of his virtue and comfort themselves with the thought that "there's something more here than is obvious." The legal system is built on the premise that the accused is "innocent until proven guilty." But few really believe that — unless you or some member of your family is the accused!

To get back to this worldview, you know there is both good and evil in the world, data that is inspiring and data that is depressing, realities that are uplifting and realities that pull you down into the depths. Intellectually or philosophically you know that both are there — like the half-fullness and the half-emptiness of the cup — but you can focus upon the one, even while acknowledging the other. And if you choose to focus on fullness instead of the emptiness of life, then what you get will be what you expect.

That doesn't mean there will be no negativity, no emptiness, no evil — it will be there aplenty. It means you will expect the positive, the fullness of life, and the good to be no less in evidence. And you will consciously choose to focus on the latter, because that is what you want out of life and that's what you want to find in your world.

When Larry was a seminary student and Norman Vincent Peale's *Power of Positive Thinking* was so popular with the public, it was fashionable among clerics and theologs to look down their noses at it because it was too "naive," too "simplistic," and (we hated to admit) too "popular" and "profitable." Why is it we never considered that negativity was equally naive, too simplistic, too popular and too profitable? So we attacked the excesses of Peale's concept as if we had therefore demolished the central idea of it. Similarly we continued preaching a message of gloom and doom as if that were the only accurate interpretation of Christianity — a feat that, in retrospect, required an act of selective exegetical sleight-of-hand.

In the last several decades, both of us have experienced increasing evidence for the power of the positive and the positively-oriented life. We find today that there are many in the medical profession who enthusiastically testify to the importance of a positive attitude in fighting and overcoming illness. Scores of clinical studies have demonstrated that the outlook of the patient is a critical factor and sometimes the most critical factor of all.

In working in the field of ESP and parapsychology, we have noted in our personal experience what researchers have repeatedly found in the laboratory: people who believe that ESP works are more likely to be able to do it than those who do not. In motivational research there have been similar findings: people are more likely to be able to perform a task when they already believe they can do it. In stress research it has been discovered that people who handle stress best are those who approach stressor experience with a positive attitude, regarding it as a challenge to be overcome, rather than as a threat that is likely to prevail.

Perhaps nowhere has the power of the positive been more apparent than in counseling people with various personal problems — physical, mental, relational, spiritual. Often this has manifested in a negative manner, for the large number of our counselees have been people whose general negative view of life is surpassed only by a specific negative view of themselves. Manifested in many different ways and reflecting diverse causes, the basic problem has usually been one of low self-esteem. Low self-esteem, in our experience, has generally come in two different packages:

1) The Born Loser — Born that way, he or she believes this is the destiny for which he or she was born. Some of these people take a perverse kind of pride in being so hopeless and worthless. No one, not even God, can help.

2) The Egotist — This person, perceived by others as being too self-confident, is often the direct opposite. Being basically insecure, he or she is constantly trying to prove to be better than his or her inner self-image.

Both "the egotist" and "the born loser" tend to think of themselves as "victims." If instead they felt in any sense that they were "victors," you may be sure they wouldn't be so miserable.

Pat Norris worked with a group of prisoners, testing the use of guided imagery and biofeedback in effecting a change of self-image. Describing the prisoners with whom she worked, she is quoted by Elmer and Alyce Green:

> I expected to find hardened men, exploitive and tough, who consciously had decided to get theirs the easy way, live off society, make it rich, and so on. Instead, I was finding fearful, angry, guilt-ridden, and impulsive people . . . mostly young who perceived themselves as failures, who felt inadequate and had very low self-esteem, and who, most significantly, perceived themselves and were perceived by others in numerous studies as victims! Victims of society, cultural deprivation, poor education and lack of opportunity, broken homes and alcoholic parents, abusive treatment and chaotic instability. . . . Victims of their own defenses, of their identifications, of their self-defeating and self-destructing behaviour, of tension and anxiety and low frustration tolerance and poor impulse control . . . [1]

If you have low self-esteem, you are preoccupied with yourself and have little or nothing left over for others. You are constantly engaged in a search for feeling better about who you are or fulfilling your own worst estimates of your inferiority. You are an egotist, not because you think too much of yourself, but because you think too little and thus you have time for nothing else but your negative image.

Some people have consistently confused low self-esteem with humility. But they are not the same, and they are not even very close. Only a person who has a sense of self-worth can be humble. The humble person has worth to lose or to offer. You can't offer or lose what you don't have. The low self-worth person is so vulnerable that anything and everything is a threat—even the smallest of mistakes, slights, or embarrass-

---

[1]Elmer and Alyce Green, *Beyond Biofeedback* (New York: Dell, 1977), p. 190. Used by permission.

ments threaten to obliterate you completely. Therefore, you find it hard to admit you are wrong (one failure, no matter how small, is intolerable), and it is almost impossible to apologize. You will also find it hard to serve others — unless you have little choice — because serving others is threatening to your eggshell ego. To the contrary, although he knew he was the Son of God, Jesus could be humble and did not find it demeaning to serve others, even to wash the feet of his disciples.

Low self-esteem is a conviction of your own lack of worth and it may represent self-dislike and even self-hatred. It is a perception that you are deficient in the very qualities that you esteem most. You can see this lack of self worth in the Four Horsemen of the Apocalypse, who are named *Defeated, Defective, Deserted, and Deprived.* You approach life negatively because your view of yourself is negative and your world is simply a projection of an overriding negativity.

Once again, we have found that some of these people will say, "But that's the way I am — what do you want me to do, close my eyes and pretend I am something else?" And our answer is usually, "As a matter of fact, that's just what we want you to do, except that you don't have to pretend you are something else, because you are — even if you don't know it."

Now you are back where you started at the beginning of this chapter, for once more you are confronted with a choice of perspectives. Yes, there is plenty that is negative in each of you. The Judeo-Christian concept calls it "sin," but it really doesn't matter what you call it. The Biblical view of human nature contains both the grandeur of the divine image in you and the misery of willful disobedience. It affirms that there is much that is distressing, but also that there is much that is inspiring. Once again, both are there, it is just a question of where you will put your attention.

So, any view of yourself as no good, unworthy, defective, and so forth, is a distorted perspective of who and what you are. It is a distortion of reality, a warped cognition, and it distorts and warps all your other perceptions and attitudes. It is an overreaction to your finitude. As David Burns, M.D., puts it, "it magnifies a trivial mistake into a symbol of major disaster." [2]

Not only does it distort your self-perception and your view of the world, but it also may distort the perceptions of other people when they look at you. You may be so persuasive in presenting yourself as "the born loser" that others set aside their own good judgment and "buy" yours. This is a vicious cycle because you will see your distorted image reflected in their eyes and find your own distortion "confirmed."

Burns tells us that research indicates that during periods of depression, people actually lose some of their capacity for clear thinking. Sometimes their thinking disorders are not dissimilar to those of schizophrenics. The evidence presented in defense of our own sense of worthlessness, says Burns, is usually irrational thinking. The low-esteem person is reporting accurately what he or she is "seeing," but it is the "seeing" itself that is distorted.

Obviously, if you are going to change this distorted picture of yourself, it is nothing you can get from a pill or a machine — no matter how exotic with all its blinking lights and readouts — nor is your distorted perspective something that can be removed with the surgeon's scalpel. Others can be of help in confirming, or at least accepting, your new self-image, but no one can give it to you. Only you can lift the veil of negativity and see what has been there from the beginning: a self that is okay, that has been there since birth or before, and that is strong enough and good enough in its essence so no negative realities can keep it from redemption when you accept it.

This doesn't mean that you need to close your eyes to the tremendous evil in the world or in yourself. The Holocaust and all our other human barbarities will not go away if you blink

---

[2]David Burns, *Feeling Good, the New Mood Therapy* (New York: Signet, 1982), p. 55.

Table 1.   The Hegerty Self-Esteem Scale

1.	I often feel inadequate to handle new situations.
2.	I habitually condemn myself for my mistakes and shortcomings.
3.	I have a driving need to prove my worth and excellence.
4.	I am much concerned with what others think or say.
5.	I am prone to condemn others and wish them punished.
6.	I tend to belittle my own talents, possessions, and achievements.
7.	I feel quite vulnerable to others' opinions, comments and attitudes.
8.	I am a professional people-pleaser.
9.	I have a deep need to gossip about others.
10.	I often blame others for my mistakes, handicaps and problems.
11.	I am a compulsive perfectionist.
12.	I customarily judge my self-worth by personal comparison with others.[3]

your eyes. But neither will the positive, constructive, and redemptive realities go away either. Once again, you must choose where you will focus your attention. What about your self-esteem? Try yourself out on the self-analysis scale in Table 1.

According to Christopher Hegerty, if you had more than a few "yes" answers to the questions, you have a "self esteem deficiency." If you do, it is time for you to decide whether you want to go through life viewing the cup of your life as "half-empty" or "half-full." If you want to see yourself in terms of emptiness instead of fullness, go ahead, it's your choice. But

---

[3]Philip Goldberg, *Executive Health* (New York: McGraw-Hill, 1978), pp. 110–111. Used by permission.

don't go belly-aching through life about the way things are — the way *you* are — because it is really just the way you choose to see yourself!

If you are a religious person, you have to realize that such a choice is the worst kind of blasphemy against your God, for you are, in effect, accusing God of being a lousy Creator — uncaring or inept or both. You are insulting the assurance that you were created "in God's image." If you are not religious and do not believe in God, you must see your negative outlook on life as an insult against all human nature, an arrogant belief that the cosmos somehow selected you to be something less than fully human. Whatever your philosophy, your ideology, your outlook on life, know that no one can make you feel inferior. If you feel that way, it's something you've done to yourself.

But take heart! If you did it to yourself, you can also *undo* it. The glass is 50 percent full and 50 percent empty. Its fullness or emptiness is simply a matter of how you choose to see it. And what you choose to see is what you get.

HOW CAN YOU CHOOSE FULLNESS INSTEAD OF EMPTINESS?

Regarding life as either empty or full is pretty much a matter of habit. Once hooked on looking on the dark side of life, we will tend to look for the dark instead of the light and surround ourselves with negativity. So, if we decide to focus on the fullness instead of the emptiness of life, we need to change our thinking habits and surround ourselves with that which is positive and constructive. For example, make a determined effort to balance your reading of the daily newspaper and viewing of television news with some authentic "good news" literature. (See the Resources at the end of this chapter for suggestions.) If thinking negatively has been a habit of many years, you may want to try Emmett Fox's "7-Day Mental Diet."[4]

In order to get a more balanced view of yourself, make a Personal Balance Sheet, dividing one or more pieces of paper into two columns: assets and liabilities. If you habitually tend to see the glass as half-empty, spend four times as much on the assets side to compensate for your habitual sensitivity to your negativities. The items on the balance sheet should be more personal than strictly financial. Once you have made your Personal Balance Sheet, run a Reality Audit on the liability side. Add the following three columns to your Personal Balance Sheet and check each liability in one of them.

a) I WAS BORN THIS WAY

b) I LEARNED TO BE THIS WAY

c) I CAN CHANGE THIS BY. . . .

You can use Dr. Norman Shealy's "Self-Love Exercise" daily. The following meditation exercise will be helpful as you will be forced to say something positive about yourself!

> Relax. Close your eyes. Take a deep breath and relax. Now repeat after me each phrase. (Pause 15 seconds after each.)
> My arms and legs are heavy and warm. (3 times)
> My heartbeat is calm and regular. (3 times)
> My body breathes itself. (3 times)
> My abdomen is warm. (3 times)
> My forehead is cool. (3 times)
> My mind is quiet and still. (3 times)
> I am at peace.
> I am very happy. (4 times)

---

[4]Emmett Fox, *Power Through Constructive Living* (New York: Harper & Row, 1940).

I succeed in my greatest desires. (4 times)
Every day in every way I am becoming more and more healthy. (4 times)
I have a very healthy and happy mind. (4 times)
I have a very healthy and loving mind. (4 times)
I am building a beautifully functioning body and mind. (4 times)
I love and appreciate all my excellent abilities. (4 times)
I know that my innermost being is magnificent, wise, and loving. (4 times)
I love and appreciate the universal life force which sustains me. (4 times)
Each time I practice these exercises, I gain more of my desires.
Every day in every way I am becoming more and more healthy.

Now as I prepare to return to my normal awareness, I feel myself bringing with me the health, happiness, comfort, and love I feel and see. I take another deep breath — eyes open — wide open — feeling happy and refreshed, feeling the energy flowing into all parts of my body.[5]

RESOURCES FOR FURTHER STUDY AND SELF-DEVELOPMENT

Magazines of Inspiration
Guideposts, 747 Third Avenue, New York, NY 10017. Monthly inspirational magazine.

---

[5]C. Norman Shealy, M.D., *The Pain Game* (Millbrae, CA: Celestial Arts, 1976), pp. 118–199. Used by permission.

Daily Word, Unity School of Christianity, Unity Village, MO
64065. Monthly devotional magazine.

The Upper Room, 1908 Grand Avenue, Nashville, TN 37202.
Monthly devotional magazine.

Books of Inspiration

Daily Readings From the Works of Leslie D. Weatherhead. Selected by
Frank Cumbers, Nashville: Abingdon Press, 1968.

Light From Many Lamps. Selected and with Commentary by
Lillian Eichler Watson, New York: Simon & Schuster,
1971.

The Choice is Always Ours. Edited by Dorothy Berkley Phillips,
Elizabeth Boyden Howes, and Lucille M. Nixon, Re-
Quest Books paperback, 1975.

*Spiritual Insights for Daily Living: A Daybook of Reflections on Ancient
Spiritual Truths of Relevance for Our Contemporary Lives.*
Edited by Elizabeth W. Fenske, Independence, Mis-
souri: Spiritual Frontiers Fellowship, 1986.

Other Resources for this Chapter:

Althouse, Lawrence W. *Rediscovering the Gift of Healing.* York
Beach, ME: Samuel Weiser, 1983, Chapter 12.

Althouse, Larry & Valere. *You CAN Save Your Breast.* New York:
W.W. Norton, 1982, Chapter 9.

Fox, Emmett. *Around the Year with Emmett Fox.* New York:
Harper & Row, 1958.

_____. *The Emmett Fox Treasury.* New York: Harper & Row,
1979.

_____. *Find and Use Your Inner Power.* New York: Harper &
Row, 1941.

_____. *Power Through Constructive Living.* New York: Harper &
Row, 1940.

Goldberg, Philip. *Executive Health.* New York: McGraw-Hill,
1978, Chapter 5.

Hoke, James H. *I Would if I Could and I Can.* Briarcliff Manor,
NY: Stein & Day, 1980, Chapters 4–15.

Peale, Norman Vincent. *The Power of Positive Thinking.* Englewood Cliffs, NJ: Prentice-Hall, 1952.

_____. *A Guide to Confident Living.* Englewood Cliffs, NJ:
Prentice-Hall, 1948.

Schuler, Robert H. *Self Esteem: The New Reformation.* Waco,
TX: Word, 1982.

CHAPTER

LEARN
TO
RELAX

Some things you learn too well. Like tensing your muscles in response to stress. You may consciously or unconsciously imitate what you see someone else doing in the same or similar circumstances, but you really don't need a teacher. You can learn these bad habits all by yourself. And, although you may soon forget how to do solid geometry or the rules of grammar, your muscles never forget the bad habits you teach them. In fact, the only way you can get them to give up those harmful old habits is to teach them some new ones — and that's what this chapter is all about: to send your muscular system back to school.

Actually, it's not quite that easy. Once you've taught your muscles some new habits — relaxing ones — you will probably find that for the rest of your life you will need to be vigilant in order to keep the old habits from taking over again. It seems you never really forget those old habits, so the trick is to keep your muscles occupied with the new, more beneficial ones.

What's wrong with those old habits is not that they are "old," but that they are destructive to our mental and physical well-being. Some tensing of muscles under certain kinds of stress is normal and even necessary. If you are in physical danger, of course you need to make your body ready for some kind of self-preserving action. This is commonly called the fight-or-flight response, a name lately given to the body's biochemical programming inherited from your prehistoric ancestors. When confronted by any danger, your ancestors learned to prepare automatically to either fight or run (flight).

Unfortunately, your body is still programmed to respond in that same manner when you are threatened or challenged today. The problem is that today it is usually inappropriate to respond to most challenges with either fight or flight. Regrettably, your body doesn't seem to realize that the boss doesn't represent the same threat to you that a dinosaur posed to your cave-dwelling ancestors. Nevertheless, despite the inappropriateness of it all, whether your challenge today is a race with the clock or a telephone that never stops ringing, your body is still reacting in the same old way: a neurological alarm message is sent throughout the body by the sympathetic and parasympathetic nervous systems, triggering an urgent chemical response from the adrenal glands into the bloodstream (adrenalin) and signalling the hypothalamus to activate the body's endocrinological control center, the pituitary gland, to call forth a whole complex of hormonal and glandular responses — whether you need them or not! Even worse for your physical and emotional health, if, instead of taking an impulsive swing at the antagonist (animal, mineral or vegetable) or running away with a loud "I quit!," you simply stand there, grinning and bearing it. Your body will probably interpret this lack of physical response as a call for even more emergency mobilization — resulting in more wear and tear.

One of the bodily systems that reacts to this ancient fight or flight programming is the musculoskeletal complex. The problem is not that the muscles react to this electrochemical call to arms (if they didn't, you'd have another kind of trouble), but that you may teach them to overreact. Your muscles get ready to propel you at an attacker when you're not going anywhere. Today, your response may be disproportionate to the stimulus.

So, your muscles not only tense unnecessarily, but very often they stay tensed long after the highly-magnified and distorted "danger" is over — hours, days, weeks, even years. And what's the harm of that? Plenty! To be specific: overly-tensed muscles do the following:

- divert your attention and disturb your powers of concentration;

- restrict the circulation of blood;

- wastefully expend energy, unnecessarily and prematurely tiring you;

- stress the nervous system, making it work longer and harder than it needs to or should;

- negatively affect memory;

- reduce the flow of visual ideas;

- restrict creativity;

- adversely affects your vision.

And what is true for the body's muscles is no less true for the other systems and organs: keep them unnecessarily running in a state of arousal and you not only sap your body's vitality, but you hasten the fatal wear-and-tear on the body itself. Turn on your carpet sweeper and let the motor run for several days without either using it or turning it off, and you will have understandably hastened the day when it wears out or needs repair.

As we have said earlier in this chapter, one of the worst aspects of this phenomenon is that it is very often taking place in your body without your even being aware of it. Eventually, you will feel the overall debilitating effect of it, although being quite unaware of the process itself.

Okay, that's the bad news. Now for the good news. The good news is that, using nothing or little more than your own human inner potential, you can gain awareness of what is going on inside you and consciously take charge of your body, including its fight or flight system.

The means of achieving this is called relaxation, and there are a number of simple techniques you can learn to accomplish it. Relaxation is the key, because, if you are completely relaxed, it is impossible for you to be tense. The two are simply incompatible. Another interesting fact is that if you learn to relax the muscular system, it affects not only the muscles, but the other systems of the body, and ultimately your state of mind. We're not really sure why that is, but it does seem to work — another demonstration of the body-mind-spirit connection. Many of the people we've counseled over the years have experienced substantial relief and help with a wide variety of physical, psychological, and spiritual disturbances just through the mastery of some simple relaxation techniques, finding that what they really needed was already within themselves, although locked away behind a wall of nervous tension.

Before you learn some of the simple muscle relaxation techniques, you need to consider a related therapeutic discipline — deep breathing. We realize that may not sound very exciting or exotic to you, but it's hard to overestimate the therapeutic value of this simple-sounding technique. Often the results of retraining the breathing habits of our counselees have been just short of miraculous.

Everyone knows two of the three functions of breathing: (1) to fill the lungs with oxygen, and (2) to expel carbon dioxide waste from the body. What you may not know or have forgotten is that breathing (3) sends life-giving oxygen to all the body tissues through the bloodstream. Despite what it may seem when you hold your breath, the lungs are not the reason you breathe, they are only the means. Breathing is an essential function of the respiratory/circulatory system, which itself is absolutely essential to health and well-being, not to mention life itself.

You have probably seen athletes on television inhaling pure oxygen on the field during a time-out or on the sidelines. This, you can be assured, is not some meaningless ritual, but an effective technique for restoring their muscles and increasing mental alertness. When you breathe deeply enough, your body benefits in a number of measurable ways: (1) your cells are revitalized, (2) your lungs are strengthened, (3) your heart burns oxygen more efficiently.

Actually, there are other beneficial effects of deep breathing. For one thing, deep breathing is an important part of any technique for relaxation, and that is the reason why it is included in this chapter. Very often, relaxation can be accomplished by deep breathing alone.

There are other benefits, too. Several years ago on a visit to Mexico City, Valere was having considerable difficulties with leg cramps. One day as we were walking through Mexico City's fine Museum of Anthropology, an idea seemed to bubble up from Larry's unconscious mind. It was as if the problem had been worked upon in the depths of his unconscious mind, surfacing only when the solution was ready to be presented *in toto*. Without stopping to think what he was saying, he turned to Valere and said: "Look, it's a problem of Mexico City's mile-high altitude — your leg muscles aren't getting enough oxygen. Whenever you feel the pains, just stop and do some deep breathing!"

This little piece of husbandly advice seemed so simplistic and unpremeditated that he was immediately sorry he had made the suggestion. But Valere, not realizing his uncertainty, began to do some deep breathing and found that it worked! And it continues to work for us and has worked for others.

Deep breathing, we have found, also has been very helpful in the management of aches and pains (particularly, but not exclusively, muscular discomfort), fatigue, controlling the emotions—try it on anger, anxiety and fear!—inducing sleep, and preparation for what could appear to be intimidating tasks—speaking in public, making a report, handling a confrontation, a dramatic or musical performance, and stimulating creativity.

Several years ago, Larry was making a flight in a little commuter airline plane. It was an extremely hot, humid day and there seemed to be little or no air conditioning in the tiny plane. Larry, who on a few occasions has experienced mild claustrophobia, began to feel he had to "get out," although it was obvious that that was hardly possible under the circumstances. Desperate, anxiety rising with every labored breath, he remembered that deep breathing and relaxation were supposed to have the effect of shutting down the body's systems to a minimal maintenance level. Since he could not "get out" physically, he would have to escape mentally. With no assurance that it would do the trick, he began to breathe deeply and slowly, telling himself to "relax . . . relax . . . relax." He could actually feel an almost immediate response from his body. It wasn't that the heat and humidity went away, but that he became increasingly detached from them. His anxiety steadily decreased and when the plane landed a half-hour later, he was completely relaxed and in control of himself.

We have found that many people habitually breathe much too shallowly. One authority says we use on the average only one-third of our lung capacity. For most of you, your lungs can hold eight times as much air as you breathe in. If you don't normally breathe deeply enough, you provide only limited, inadequate amounts of oxygen to your body and do not fully rid your body of carbon dioxide and other wastes.

Deep breathing exercises not only can improve your health in general, but also can: (1) strengthen the heart and lungs, (2) reduce anxiety (general and specific), (3) reduce anger and resentment, (4) produce feelings of mastery and/or self-control, (5) eliminate some types of fatigue, (6) reduce muscle tension. One of the reasons people may be dubious about the value of deep breathing is that it sounds too easy, too commonplace. You may find, however, that the following techniques are neither.

HOW CAN YOU RETRAIN YOUR BREATHING HABITS?

In all breathing techniques it's important to push the air out of your lungs with your diaphragm. Otherwise, you don't properly empty and fill them. To make certain that you're using your diaphragm, place one of your hands on it so you can feel it move in and out as you inhale and exhale. Posture is also very important, so either sit erect (preferably in a hard, straight chair), or lie down. Some people are too prone (pun unintended) to fall asleep if they lie down. Regardless of which position you choose, your spine should be straight and your diaphragm unencumbered by chest or stomach.

In some yoga breathing techniques, you are instructed to breathe in through your nose, and exhale through your mouth. This is optional, but helpful to many.

Test your lung capacity by breathing in very slowly until you can't take in any more air. While you are doing this, direct your attention to your lungs and be very aware of your present capacity to inhale. Then exhale and follow the same procedure. These limits are, of course, not your normal breathing practice, but demonstrate the deeper capacities which you must use in your breathing techniques. The following exercise is the basic breathing technique.

Eight In, Eight Out

Using a tempo of one count every half-second, breathe in very slowly and deeply to the count of 8. Then, just as deliberately and slowly, exhale to the count of 8. Your breathing must be very even and smooth. While you are doing this exercise, focus all your attention on your breathing, as if there were nothing else of importance in the world but the act of breathing in and breathing out. Practice this exercise in cycles of 10 full breaths (in and out). Keep working on this exercise until you can slow the tempo and maintain a smooth, even breath.

This simple (although not always easy) technique can be exceptionally effective for relaxation, calming your nerves, releasing tension, improving concentration, and gaining personal control over yourself.

The Inverted Triangle

This is an advanced technique to use when you have mastered the *Eight-In, Eight-Out* technique. The difference from the above technique is that after you have inhaled to the count of 8, you hold your breath to the count of 4, before exhaling to the count of 8. Practice this in cycles of 10 full inhalations-holds-exhalations. Remember to concentrate fully on your breathing.

The Rectangle

This technique takes even more concentration and can be extremely effective. Inhale slowly and deeply to the count of 8, hold your breath for the count of 4, exhale to the count of 8, and hold your emptied breath to the count of 4. Do in cycles of 10, but don't be surprised if you find yourself getting lost between the first and tenth round. This is what makes it so effective for concentration. Let the technique totally absorb your attention.

The Square

This technique is for truly advanced students of breathing control. It is similar to the Rectangle above, except that you hold your breath both times to the count of 8 instead of 4.

HOW CAN WE LEARN TO RELAX?

Have you ever been awakened in the middle of the night with a cramp in your leg or foot? If you have, did you stop to ponder that, at a time when supposedly you were in a deep state of relaxation, you were caused pain by an overtensed muscle? Actually, that's not as strange as it may seem. Much of the time, even when we think we are reasonably relaxed, there is, in some part of our body, muscle tension that we are unaware of. This is called "residual tension," tension that resides in your body. Take a quick mental inventory of your body to see if there are any areas where there is unnecessary muscle tension: neck? shoulders? arms? hands? fingers? legs? feet? toes? Controlled relaxation can help. It is sometimes regarded as a fad of the past few decades, but various techniques, particularly yoga, have been with us for thousands of years.

While a student at Harvard in 1908, Edmund Jacobson became aware of the "residual tension" phenomena. Throughout his career as a physician-physiologist, Dr. Jacobson studied the relaxation and tension of muscles, eventually devising a technique, progressive relaxation, to teach people how to completely relax their muscles. Jacobson discovered that the more able his students became in learning to relax muscle groups, the more they relaxed mentally and felt relaxed inside. Jacobson used his progressive relaxation technique to successfully treat a wide range of physical disorders, including anxiety, ulcers, hypertension and insomnia.

The original Jacobson technique was very time-consuming, requiring 60 hours of training during which students learned to relax 39 separate muscle groups. This original technique has been much abbreviated and modified since the 1930s when he first introduced it, so that today one can learn progressive relaxation much more simply and quickly.

Progressive Relaxation

This is a technique that is our adaptation of the Jacobson program. It is one of the most effective means of relaxing your body and producing a meditative state of passive alertness. In addition to releasing nervous tension, and producing a sense of self-control, it is invaluable in strengthening your powers of concentration.

Follow these steps:

1) Review the instructions for the breathing techniques on page 35.

2) Keeping in mind what you have learned in the *Eight-In, Eight-Out* breathing technique, close your eyes and breathe in and out to the slow count of 8. As you exhale, say to yourself: "Relax . . . relax . . . relax." Do this three times, making sure the breathing is deep, slow and even.

3) Continue to breathe deeply and slowly and concentrate on your breathing. As you do, let go of all tension in your body.

4) Then, as if your mind were not restricted to the cranium, see and feel yourself reaching down with the mind and grasping the toes of your left foot. Sense the toes with your mind. Physically tense the toes, and then release the tension with both your mind and muscles, saying to yourself, "I relax and let go the toes of my left foot." Follow this same procedure in this order: left foot, lower left leg (ankle to knee), upper left leg, the right leg the same as the left, the lower torso (genitals, intestines, stomach, etc.), chest (alimentary canal, lungs, heart), back (vertebra by vertebra), fingers, hands, lower arms, upper arms (left, then right), shoulders to neck, face, back and top of head.

When you have reached the top of your head, say to yourself: "I am now fully relaxed and with each breath I take, I go deeper and deeper into relaxation."

While you are going through the above procedure, it is important to visualize your body, as well as to sense the "feel" of it with your mind. The key is to relax and let go of each part of the body in a progressive manner.

When you have mastered the progressive relaxation technique, you may use it as a prelude to any of the meditative techniques described in chapter 8.

Muscle Relaxation

There is no one right way to do relaxation. There are hundreds of variations on the above technique, as well as dissimilar techniques for obtaining similar results. Some of these techniques involve the actual movement of muscles and muscle groups for the purpose of relaxing them. You will need to experiment with various techniques to determine which are best for you.

Stretching: Sit quietly, closing your eyes and breathing deeply and slowly. With your mind, explore your body to determine where there are tensions being held. Now, stand up and, like a cat, stretch slowly, gracefully, luxuriently. As you do this, continue to breathe deeply and feel the tension leave your body. Then, with a deep sigh, exhale, feeling the last of the tension leave your body, and sit down in a relaxed and passive state. Savor this feeling for a few minutes.

Shaking: Stand up with your arms hanging loosely at your side. Begin by shaking just your hands (not moving the rest of your arms). Then, in a few seconds, add the lower arms, then the upper arms, and then your shoulders. Concentrate on the feeling of vibration and energy. Gradually decrease the shaking until you have completely stopped, and feel the tingling in your body. Now, go through the same procedure with your feet and legs.

Palming: This is particularly good for eyes that are tired and strained — much better than rubbing them. First, blink your eyes a few times to lubricate them. With your fingers, briefly massage your temples and then the nape of your neck. Now, close your eyes and cup your palms over them, so that there is no weight or pressure on the eyeballs, but just on the bone of the eye sockets. Now, occupy your mind with the most pleasant scenes you can imagine. While you do this with the "inner" or "mind's eye," you do not stare or strain the eyes to do so. For a while, your inner field of eye vision will contain colors or glimmers of light. When your visual field has become black, your eyes are fully relaxed.

Self-Massage: As we are writing these words, we have been waiting for our masseuse to come to our room to give us massages. After sitting at a typewriter all day, we look forward to the relaxation the massage always brings. Just moments ago, she called to cancel her appointment with us. How timely, therefore, to be in the act of telling you how to do a self-massage, the next best thing.

You can do the self-massage sitting in a chair. Use your own hands gently, but firmly. Do not exert so much pressure that it causes you pain. Using your palms and fingertips in a circular motion as if you were rubbing in some kind of cream or lotion, start at the top of your head and move downward over your face, the back of your head, down the neck, shoulders, chest and stomach. Linger with your hands wherever you feel you need more massage. Use your left hand to massage the right hand and arm, including fingers. Then use your right hand on the left side. Use both hands on your lower back, moving up the back as far as you can reach. You can apply more pressure at various points, when it feels safe to do so — but do not massage too hard. Then, massage the pelvic region, the buttocks, hips and upper and lower legs, one leg at a time. Finish with the ankles, feet and toes.

Autogenic Training Techniques

Autogenic training is a systematic series of training exercises developed by Johannes H. Schultz in the early 1900s to teach patients a systematic means of self-regulation or gaining conscious control over their bodies. Schultz was a psychiatrist and neurologist in Berlin and his work in Autogenics has been carried on by his student, Dr. Wolfgang Luthe. Quite popular and recognized in Europe, particularly among members of the medical profession, autogenic training is also becoming better known in the United States.

The first autogenic training exercise can be a very effective method for relaxation training. The following technique is adapted from that method:

1) Sit comfortably and straight in a chair with your hands in your lap, your legs uncrossed and your body straight. Close your eyes.

2) Take a few long, deep breaths and relax . . . relax . . . relax.

3) Let your mind come to a state of passive attention.

4) Let your mind focus passively on the arm you use most.

5) Say to yourself: "My right (or left) arm is heavy." Pause ten seconds, then say it again, until you have paused and said it ten times.

6) Then break the mood and this state of mind by stirring, moving your body, opening your eyes and flexing your limbs. You will note that some of the feeling of "heaviness" stays with your arm. The period of stirring and movement in step 6 is to help your mind and body distinguish between the different states.

7) Then repeat steps 4, 5, and 6 four more times. Each time take note of the physical sensations in your arm. They may spread to your other limbs.

8) Focus on the other arm, now, and continue until both arms feel heavy.

Relaxation Through Visualization

In chapter 9 we will be dealing at length with imagery and visualization techniques. Following is a visualization technique that you may find effective when it's obvious that your physical tension is closely tied to anxiety, worry, or strong emotions. Instead of speaking directly to muscles and muscle groups, as in progressive relaxation, in this exercise you are using mental images to quiet the inner turmoil, which will also tend to relax the body as well.

Water is frequently symbolic of human emotions. There-fore visualize a large body of water — lake, sea or ocean — in the grips of a raging storm. Image howling winds, torrential down-pours, and turbulent waves. Watch the storm rise in intensity and then, as its energy is expended, observe as the storm begins to diminish — winds, rain and waves. Watch the energy of the body of water gradually diminish until the surface of the water becomes calm . . . and even serene with hardly a ripple or swell.

For those with a background in Christianity, the story of Jesus calming the storm on the Sea of Galilee (Mark 4:35-41) may be a helpful variation on this technique.

This technique demonstrates once again how interrelated are the body, the mind and the emotions. If your body is tense, it is unlikely that you will experience inner peace. If, on the other hand, your body is deeply relaxed, it will be difficult to sustain a high level of anxiety. In chapter one we were con-cerned with kicking the worry habit; it is virtually impossible to be deeply relaxed in your body and to continue worrying. In the next chapter we will be looking at ways to cope with stress; there are many techniques and strategies, but guided or self-induced relaxation is one of the most important.

Actually, these and other drugless means of relaxation should be our first line of defense against needless tension and stress. They are generally more effective than drugs and quite without the disturbing side effects of tranquilizers — including addiction. (We'll have more to say on this in chapter 6 when we consider sleep problems and techniques.) Unfortunately, tranquilizers do not help us solve our problems; they give us temporary relief from caring about them. All too often, however, those who come to crave that temporary relief become hooked on it and use more and more drugs to keep their problems hidden from the conscious mind. Relaxation techniques are not designed to hide your concerns — not even temporarily — but to help you gain control over your feelings so that you can face and resolve your problems and meet your challenges.

Learning to relax can be one of the most important skills at your disposal for dealing with life's negativities and helping you accentuate the positive.

RESOURCES FOR FURTHER STUDY AND SELF-DEVELOPMENT

Benson, Herbert, M.D., with Klipper, Miriam Z. *The Relaxation Response.* New York: William Morrow, 1976.

Ebon, Martin. *The Relaxation Controversy.* New York: Signet paperback, 1976.

Shealy, C. Norman, M.D. *90 Days to Self-Health.* New York: Dial Press, 1977, Chapters 6 and 10.

White, John and Fadiman, James, eds. *Relax: How You Can Feel Better, Reduce Stress, and Overcome Tension.* New York: Confucian Press, 1976.

CHAPTER

STRESS:
TURNING LEMONS
INTO LEMONADE

It was almost twenty years ago that Larry's physician told him that he had a serious case of arthritis. His doctor said that it was a condition that would grow steadily worse; there was nothing he could do but accept it and learn to live with it while taking medication to alleviate the pain. Although the prognosis came as somewhat of a shock, the diagnosis itself was not surprising to Larry. For several years he had been aware of a gradually worsening discomfort in some of his joints and limbs. After driving for fifteen or twenty minutes, he began to find it uncomfortable to open the door and get out of the car. It took several seconds before he could stand completely upright, and even then he might walk for a bit from a slightly bent position. There were also times when, if he placed his arm over the back of a chair, he would have to literally pick it up with his other hand in order to move it. Worst of all, his body ached so much that he was unable to get a good night's sleep. The gradual intensification of these symptoms eventually led him to the doctor's office.

He expected the doctor would tell him he had arthritis. What he had not expected was the prognosis that there was nothing to be done for it, and that it was a gradually deteriorating condition. Although he respected his physician's competence and assumed that, medically speaking, he was quite correct, Larry decided then and there that he was not about to accept the doctor's prognostication.

He began to ask himself what in his lifestyle might have caused, or at least contributed to, this condition. It didn't take long to decide that one reason might well be his failure to manage his stress adequately. It might not be apparent to others, but he was aware that the pressures of his work as a busy pastor took a substantial inner toll from him. He decided that it was imperative to learn to relax, to stop worrying, to learn to handle his daily tasks without letting obstacles become major inner conflicts. He began a daily program of relaxation, meditation, and visualization techniques. The result: less than two years later he was completely free of all arthritic symptoms and has remained free ever since.

We can't prove scientifically that Larry healed himself of arthritis through relaxation, meditation, and visualization. But we can say with certainty that the diminishment and eventual disappearance of arthritic symptoms was concurrent with a growing capacity to deal with daily tensions—and without the benefit of either medication or medical therapy. Ironically, Larry now realizes that if his physician had given him a prescription for an effective medication, he probably would not have made any of the important changes within himself that he now believes needed to be made.

Today we know a great deal more about stress, what it is, and how it affects us physically, mentally, and spiritually. Stress, according to Dr. Hans Selye and others, is necessary to life.[1] It

---

[1]The late Dr. Hans Selye is generally regarded as one of the great medical pioneers of the 20th century and the father of research on stress. For many years, he was Professor and Director of the Institute of Experimental Medi-

spurs us on to achievement and makes life more interesting. Without it, there would be no constructive activity, no growth — either in the individual or in society in general. Actually, stress is inherently neither good nor bad, but depends pretty much on how we view it. The same stress that makes one person ill can invigorate another.

Although most of us use the term stress indiscriminately, Dr. Selye, the pioneer in stress research, distinguishes between stress and distress, the latter referring to what he called "the rate of wear and tear" on our bodies, the price we pay for trying to cope with the changes demanded by life. "Life," says Selye, "is largely a process of adaptation to the circumstances in which we exist." It is our failure to adapt successfully that produces the destructive wear and tear on us.

What is the cost of these unsuccessful adaptations to the changes and challenges of life? The answer: billions and billions of dollars daily, and millions of lives crippled or cut short by the top four medical disorders in the industrialized societies of the world — the USA, Europe, and Japan. Cardiovascular diseases, cancer, arthritis, and respiratory diseases (including emphysema and bronchitis) are stress-related, meaning that distress plays an important role in causing and perpetuating these conditions. Some standard medical texts say that 50 percent to 80 percent of all diseases are stress-related. But other physicians, the celebrated Dr. Arnold Hutschnecker[2] for one, believe that all diseases may have some stress factor.

In the USA today, the number one disease afflicting more than twenty-four million Americans is hypertension (or high

---

cine and Surgery at the University of Montreal, and the author of 32 books and more than 1500 technical articles. Two of his works on stress are to be found in the Resource section of this chapter, page 56.

[2]Arnold Hutschnecker, M.D., a New York physician, was a pioneer in exploring the mind-body relationship as it related to physical and emotional illness. Two of his books are classics in this field: *The Will to Live* (New York: Prentice Hall, 1951), and *The Will to Happiness* (New York: Cornerstone Library, 1964).

blood pressure). Hypertension is the single most significant factor in several other serious diseases, including hardening of the arteries, strokes, congestive heart failure, kidney failure, and angina pectoris. A thirty-five-year-old person suffering from undetected and untreated hypertension can anticipate losing seventeen years from his or her life expectancy. And hypertension is very certainly a stress-related disease.

Unfortunately, many people think of stress or distress as largely imaginary or psychological — meaning, therefore, "not real." Actually, however, harmful stress is really much more physiological than it is psychological in its effects. In his early experiments with rats, Dr. Hans Selye discovered that the rodents, when subjected to stressful conditions, manifested specific physical symptoms: the enlargement of the adrenal cortex (actually the only organ that enlarges under stress), the shrinkage or atrophy of the thymus, spleen, and lymph nodes (the latter are part of the body's immune system), the disappearance of white blood cells, and bleeding ulcers. He subsequently found the same and other physical reactions in people.

So, although the perception of a threat or challenge may be imaginative or subjective, the result is both specific and physical. Close your eyes for a moment and vividly imagine being threatened by an emotionally unstable person with a knife or gun in his hand. If you have any imagination at all, these images will cause a number of chemical and neurological (electrical) responses within your body that are manifested in one or more of the following measurable physiological symptoms: increased blood pressure, heightened respiratory rate, additional motor excitability in the muscle, dilation of the pupils, additional stored fats and sugars released into the bloodstream, an increase in the presence of red blood cells, the cessation of digestion, an increase in the blood-clotting mechanisms of the body, and the loosening of bowel and bladder muscles. All of these symptoms are the immediate result of an idea of personal danger — rightly or wrongly perceived — and held in the mind! And if emotions can cause these specific physiological responses, why should we have difficulty in believing that they can also cause much more extensive physical damage in the body?

Years ago, Dr. Thomas Holmes, of the University of Washington Medical School, devised a statistical schedule of "stressor" experiences, ranking them in importance from one to thirty-seven. Number one was "death of a spouse" (rated at 100 points) followed by "divorce" (68 points), and "marital separation" (65 points), on down to "minor violations of the law" (11 points). Obviously, for most people the death of a spouse and divorce are more likely to be stressful than minor violations of the law.

Stress researchers, however, have made two very important observations about these stressor experiences. First of all, they have found that even pleasant experiences can be stressful. ("Marriage," for example, is number seven on the Holmes scale at 50 points.) But even more important is the observation that none of these stressors actually cause distress to us. What causes stressful wear and tear on us, rather, is our perception of, and reaction to, these experiences.

The key, then, in meeting the challenges of daily living is not so much what goes on *outside* us, but what goes on *inside* us. And the good news is that we can manage or control our stress because, when we are aware, we can choose how we will react to our stressor experiences. Our aim, therefore, is not so much stress avoidance, but stress management — taking conscious charge of the unrealized powers within us.

In their book, *Stress,* authors McQuade and Aikman make the observation that, according to medical science, frustration and stress damage our circulatory systems, digestive tracts, lungs, muscles and joints, and generally speed up the aging process. The authors tell us, "We don't *catch* migraines or coronary disease, or perhaps even cancer, despite the virus theory.

These sicknesses happen to us because we are rendered vulnerable by the way we choose to live."[3]

You do not have to succumb to stress because you have within you the capacity to choose how you will respond to the challenges of life. Isn't that an exciting concept? In fact, researchers have found that people who manage stress most successfully are those who respond to the stressors of life as challenges to be met and overcome. You are challenged to turn your lemons into lemonade.

WHAT CAN YOU DO ABOUT STRESS?

1) Learn and use techniques for self-regulation in this book. Some of the techniques examined and taught in other chapters are exceptionally important in learning self-regulation, particularly the relaxation techniques in chapter 3, physical mastery in chapter 5, meditation in chapter 8, and visualization in chapter 9. In addition, several other chapters (1, 2, and 12, particularly) can be helpful in learning to cope with distress.

2) Learn more about stress and the means of managing it by reading one or more of the books listed at the end of this chapter.

3) Take instruction in self-regulation through biofeedback or autogenic training. Instruction in either or both of these disciplines can be found in many cities. Note the resources listed at the end of this chapter.

4) Learn to recognize the symptoms of distress and identify your stressors. Create your own "stress journal" to chart your stressors and how you react to them. Table 2 on page 52 shows

----

[3]Walter McQuade and Ann Aikman, *Stress* (New York: Dutton, 1974), p. 6.

an example of such a stress journal. Use your own to learn when and why you are likely to react adversely (distressfully) to stress. Some of the possible physical symptoms are included in this table.

Each day examine your stress journal for patterns of distress. Some of the questions you will need to ask yourself are:

1) Are there some activities/experiences in which I am consistently manifesting symptoms of distress? Which are these?

2) Who are the people with whom I am most likely to experience distress? Why do I become distressed when I must deal with them?

3) Do any of the following hidden stressors contribute to the distress I experience in these situations: noise, uncomfortable temperatures, odors, bad lighting, uncomfortable or distracting conditions?

4) Are there clusters of stressors — two or more stressful situations in close proximity? (For example, in Table 2 note the proximity of the "irritability" and "muscle tension" experienced within the same one-hour period.) Normally, we may be able to handle individual stressors pretty well, but when they cluster in a relatively short period of time, we may have considerable trouble coping with all the changes required. Multiple stressors have a cumulative effect, like compound interest.

5) When you have identified some repetitive distressful situations, ask yourself the following questions and write out your answers.

First, consider your perception of what happened:

- Just what is it that's happening here?
- How am I perceiving this event?
- Am I seeing it pretty clearly, or am I missing something, or adding something that really isn't there?

Table 2. Stress Journal

Day	Experience	People Involved	Stress Symptom	Stress Score	Hour/ Weight	Total Pts.	Comments
7–7:30am	Breakfast	Wife/son	Irritability	3	$1/2$	$1 1/2$	Family wants to talk; I don't
7:30–8am	Drive to work	—	Muscle tension	5	$1/2$	$2 1/2$	TRAFFIC!
8–9am	Desk work	Secretary		2	1	2	
9–9:30am	Conf. with Boss		Headaches Cold sweats	5	$1/2$	$2 1/2$	Unpredictable

STRESS SCORES

1 point = Activity/experience pleasant, enjoyable and relaxing
2 points = Activity/experience pleasant, but taxing
3 points = Activity/experience necessary, but taxing (neither pleasant or unpleasant)
4 points = Activity/experience unpleasant, hurried or tension-producing
5 points = Activity/experience very unpleasant, pressured, or tension-producing

- Is it possible for me to see this situation differently? From someone else's point of view? (For example, in the sample table, our stress candidate may be seeing his family's talking at the breakfast table as a lack of respect for his privacy. Instead, he could view breakfast conversation as a genuine desire to communicate about things of some importance to family members.)

Then look at your reactions:

- How am I reacting to this situation?
- Is my response justified? (For example, do I have a right to be irritable?)
- Am I overreacting to this situation?
- Is this the only way I can respond, or are there other appropriate responses I could make?

After you have answered your questions, summarize the experience so you can learn from it. Looking again at the stressful situation, what can be changed?

- The situation?
- Significant factors in the situation?
- My attitude toward the situation?
- Several or all of the above?

Going back to the sample table, some of the following changes might be possible:

- Situation: Perhaps our stress candidate could leave for work at a time when the traffic is not so congested.
- Significant Factors: Maybe he could change the route so that, although longer, it would not be so frustrating.
- Attitude: Our stress candidate might learn to regard the time required to drive to work as an excellent opportunity to listen to some music or self-improvement tapes.

6) Look at your stressors to determine how much or how little control you may have over the situation. Professor Robert Karasek of Columbia University found, in a study he made, that people who have little control over their jobs — cooks, garment stitchers, assembly line workers — have a higher rate of heart disease. Other studies have indicated that people who feel they have sufficient control over their lives tend to handle stress more successfully.

Now that you've taken a look at your own stressors and your reactions to them, think about and answer the following questions:

- In the situations in which you experience the greatest distress, over what factors in the situation do you have the most control, in total or in part? the least control?
- In those situations are you exercising all the control that is within your power?
- If not, where and how do you need to exercise more control over these factors?

Many factors may be quite beyond your control — the actions and statements of other people, accidents, sickness, conditions of employment and so forth — but there may be enough factors within your control — how you regard these actions and words, how you interpret what is happening, the attention you give to these circumstances, and so forth — that you can keep these stressors from unduly taxing our resources.

7) Make sure your "cures" are not hidden stressors. Too many people seek escape from a hectic week of work in a hectic weekend of play. Whether they work or play, there is still a "drivenness" about them. Are any of your cures for stress themselves possible stressors? For example, do you use a lot of alcohol, narcotics, barbiturates? Are your recreational activities simply an extension of your compulsion to compete and/or prove yourself? Does your social and recreational life tend to

restore your vitality, or do these activities contribute to the drain on your vital resources? Do you allow yourself sufficient time off from stressful activities? How well do you function on a vacation?

8) Examine yourself for indications of "Type A" behavior. Type A behavior is a standard of classification of personality types pioneered by Dr.'s Meyer Friedman and Ray Rosenman. Type A people are those who are aggressively involved in a chronic, incessant struggle to achieve more and more in less and less time. Although the popular conception is that Type A people are model executives, researchers have found that Type A's are not always successful at higher-level jobs. Type B's are frequently more capable corporate managers. Type A's are three times more coronary-prone than Type B's, even B's who are smokers, who have hypertension or a family history of coronaries. Type A's discharge excess stress hormones into their bloodstreams — cortisol, epinephrine, and norepinephrine. They also have excess insulin in their blood and take three to four times longer to discharge dietary cholesterol after meals. To determine whether or not you are a Type A person, answer the following questions:

- Do you constantly try to accomplish too much in too little time?
- Do you find yourself in a constant race with the clock?
- Do you make most of your activities competitive even when you don't have to?
- Do you find yourself subject to a free-floating hostility — a sense of hostility that doesn't seem to have any specific or direct cause?

If you find yourself saying "yes" to several of the above questions, take a good, hard look at your lifestyle. Judging "good" as being "good in the long run," what is "good" about it? Using the same long run perspective, what is "bad" about it? How much of your lifestyle is necessary? Inescapable? Expendable? Changeable?

Many people consciously or unconsciously choose distress because they are unwilling to make any necessary changes in their lifestyle. According to Dr. Hans Selye, "Our goal shouldn't be to master techniques for shutting out reality, but to devise a better lifestyle."

None of us are really born with a lifestyle or decreed it by fate, karma, or any other inevitability. It is something that we are free to choose and change — if we want to. What about you: are you in charge of your lifestyle or is it in charge of you?

RESOURCES FOR FURTHER STUDY & SELF-DEVELOPMENT

Forbes, Rosalind, Ed.D. *Corporate Stress.* New York: Doubleday, 1979.

Gardner, Dr. David C. and Beatty, Dr. Grace Joely. *Stop Stress and Aging Now.* Windham, NH: American Training and Research Associates, 1985.

Levinson, Harry. *Executive Stress.* New York: Harper & Row, 1965.

McQuade, Walter and Aikman, Ann. *Stress.* New York: E.P. Dutton, 1974.

Selye, Hans. *The Stress of Life.* New York: McGraw-Hill, 1956.

Stein, Richard A., M.D. *Personal Strategies for Living With Less Stress.* New York: John Gallagher, 1983.

Woolpolk, Robert L., Ph.D. and Richardson, Frank C., Ph.D. *Stress, Sanity & Survival.* New York: Simon & Schuster, 1978.

CHAPTER

YOUR BODY:
WHO'S
IN CHARGE?

In 1977, two Nobel Prize winners, Doctors Roger C.L. Guillemin and Andrew V. Schally, proved conclusively that the human brain secretes neurohormones that control the pituitary, the master gland of the endocrine system. This means that thoughts and mental pictures can be transformed into hormones! Ideas are not just immaterial impressions in the mind, but material streams of chemicals in the physical body.

We have tended to think of ideas as some kind of "vapors of the mind," not "real" because they lacked some kind of materiality or physical form. If someone suffered an injury to an arm or leg, it was regarded as "real." At the same time, if someone else were to agonize over an "inner" pain—bereavement, disappointment, frustration and so forth—the pain of it would likely be dismissed as being "all in your mind."

Today, due to the work of Guillemin, Schally, and many others, that kind of thinking is no longer justified. Ideas are both physical and mental. Being both electrical and chemical, they have a materiality all their own. Now as never before, we are realizing the tremendous interdependence and interrelationship between the mind and the body. We may speak of body/mind as separate, but we can never really isolate the one from the other. In chapter 11 we will examine the implications of this for meeting challenges of illness and injury. But in this chapter we will look at body/mind from the perspective of personal autonomy, so we can learn to take charge of ourselves and our lives.

It's strange that we spend so much of our childhood and adolescence trying to assert and demonstrate our independence, and, then, having it within our grasp, decide that we really don't want to be in charge of anything. We allow others to take charge of our minds and our volition, while giving our bodies over to the habits and demands of our unconscious. Some of us prefer the security of spiritual servitude to the challenge and insecurity of autonomy. It's not very stimulating, but it is familiar and therefore it feels secure.

Many of the people who come to us for counseling suffer from the effects of poor self-esteem. They don't value themselves enough to make life worthwhile, or, as the Transactional Analysis people would put it, they don't feel "O.K." to be themselves. There are a number of reasons why people have low self-esteem, but one of the most frequent, we find, is that many people do not feel that they are "in control" of their own lives. They tend to feel that they are "victims." We try to challenge them to make a new "Declaration of Independence," to fight within themselves, if necessary, their own "Revolution" or "War of Independence" and to frame their own personal "Constitution" — in short: to consciously and deliberately take charge of themselves.

Many people respond well to this challenge. They are quite anxious to take charge of their minds, to rule their emotions, to guide their own destinies. If there is going to be any resistance at all, it comes when we challenge them to also take charge of their own bodies. Too many of them regard their bodies simply as necessary shells or vehicles for that part of themselves that is really important — their psyches (mind/ spirit). At best their attitude toward their bodies is one of tolerance or indifference, at worst of shame and even hostility. Although with effort and new understanding they may learn to love mind and spirit, they find it unthinkable to love the body.

But "A house divided against itself," said Jesus, "cannot stand." As Abraham Lincoln noted, when this happens to a nation, civil war is the likely result. And when this takes place within one individual life, there is an inner war that is no less costly and destructive, not to mention foolish.

You cannot really take charge of your life without being willing to assume responsibility for, and control over, your body. And it may well be that you will not really be able to love your body until you have begun to subject it to your own will.

One of the first symptoms of aging is the gradual loss of control over the body, the realization that it will no longer do what you want it to do, or what it once did (although we all tend to be somewhat idealistic in remembering what it "used to do"). You cannot keep your body from aging — although you can certainly slow down the aging process — but you can keep the body and your physical powers from slipping from your grasp long before it needs to happen.

When Larry sits down at the piano and attempts to play one of his old favorites, Chopin's E-flat Nocturne (opus 9, no. 2), he is distressed to find that, although his mind remembers what his fingers are to do, the fingers no longer appear to be willing to carry out his commands. At this point in his life, this failure is not the result of aging, but a loss of mastery over his fingers through a sheer lack of practice.

It is often true with the rest of the physical body: it no longer does what you want it to do, not just because it has aged, but because you have relinquished control over it.

We have used the last eleven paragraphs to ease into saying something you probably don't want to hear: *Taking charge of your life involves taking charge of your body — and taking charge of your body requires subjecting yourself to some form of discipline that involves a program of physical exercise.* We wouldn't for one minute say that we "like" exercise. We can't ever remember getting up one single morning and saying, "Oh boy, time to exercise!" This morning, like many mornings (and we won't tell you how many) we dreaded the thought of exercise, particularly because here in Austria, while we are writing this book, it comes *first* on our regimen. (At home in Dallas it follows breakfast, a brisk three-mile walk, meditation and prayer).

We could have thought of a thousand reasons not to exercise this morning. (If you think your mind is stagnant and uncreative, just propose a little exercise to it and watch it work!) But we determined a long time ago that we would not be ruled by our weakest and most foolish impulses. We know that we cannot avoid our program of exercise very long without losing control of our bodies, and that, we are determined, we will not do.

Actually, a well-thought-out program of exercise will pay tremendous unexpected dividends on your investment of time, self-discipline and energy. A healthy, disciplined physical body is linked to the attainment of healthy, disciplined emotions. A good program of regular exercise will help you live longer and live better.

The following list of benefits from good exercise is only a partial, albeit an impressive, list of benefits:

- *Helps us to better manage stress.* Exercise helps to release muscular tension, and dissipates the intense energies of the "fight-or-flight" response in the body in a constructive way. Dr. Hans Selye found in his stress research that under-exercised mice were more susceptible to stress and its distressing effects.

- *Gives us increased strength and endurance.* Of course, while you're doing it, you tend to think it's decreasing your strength and endurance. But not long afterward, you'll find that it adds-to rather than takes-away-from your vitality.

- *Provides for the more efficient use of energy.* Since it helps to dispel tension, improve circulation, and so forth, exercise permits you to have more energy left over for other tasks, including mental tasks.

- *Maintains proper circulation.* Stop and think for a moment how many physical problems and effects of aging are tied to poor circulation!

- *Improves muscle tone.* Many of those things you used to do that you no longer can do are the result of the loss of muscle tone.

- *Serves as an appetite suppressant.* Exercise causes the endocrine system to produce hormones which are natural suppressants of appetite: dopamine, noradrenaline, and serotonin. It is popularly assumed that vigorous exercise makes you hungry, but that is only when you have depleted your energy — and a good program of exercise increases rather than depletes your store of energy.

- *Enables improved weight control.* Not only does exercise burn calories, but it also dissipates nervous tension and stress which often, rather than appetite, are the reasons you overeat or eat unwisely.

- *Reduces chronic tiredness.* Once again, we know that may seem quite contrary to reason, but a feeling of "tiredness" is often the result, not of physical exertion, but boredom, inactivity, diminished use of the body, and stress.

- *Reduction of aches, pains, and stiffness.* Although this, too, may seem to run counter to reason and experience, we have found our positive experience with exercise confirmed by published findings from clinical trials and experience. Dr. C. Norman Shealy, a surgeon who operates a pain clinic in Springfield, Missouri, in his book, *The Pain Game* (Celestial Arts, 1976), tells of the extensive use he and his associates make of exercise programs in helping people with chronic pain of most kinds.

- *Helps to reduce serious accidents.* By helping to reduce stress and improve concentration (a frequent cause of accidents), by improvement of muscle tone, and so forth, a program of exercise has been demonstrated to reduce the incidence of serious accidents.

- *Improves appearance.* The reasons should be obvious.

- *Reduces degenerative disease factors.* Mobilizing the body's natural defense and healing systems, exercise can be an important factor.

- *Causes mood elevation.* We have frequently found that people who have a regular exercise program do not experience chronic depression. Although we have begun many an exercise session in a "down" mood, we cannot recall ever finishing a session with that same feeling of depression. The reason, we believe, is both psychological and biochemical.

- *Contributes to ego strength.* If one of the reasons you often feel "badly" about yourself is that you have not experienced the satisfaction of disciplining yourself and accomplishing a desired objective, then conversely, when you have achieved something with yourself — such as a period of exercise — you feel "good" about yourself — stronger, more worthy.

- *Dissipates strong, harmful emotions such as anger and hostility.* If you doubt that, wait until the next time you're about to have a temper tantrum or "explode" at someone and then, instead, do a half-hour program of exercise that includes aerobics.

- *Relieves boredom.*

- *Makes relaxation considerably easier and therefore enhances any activity that is dependent upon relaxation.*

- *Induces restful sleep.* Hold that pill! Try running in place instead!

- *Produces some direct physical benefits:*

Lowers blood pressure;

Lowers resting heart rate (so heart doesn't have to work as hard to distribute blood to the rest of body);

Increases cardiac input, improving its ability to circulate blood under stress;

Increases number of red blood cells, improving supply of oxygen;

Increases elasticity of arteries;

Lowers triglyceride level;

Decreases blood cholesterol level, achieving better balance of high and low density cholesterol;

Diminishes secretions of adrenal glands in response to stress;

Diminishes lactic acid in the muscles, decreasing fatigue and tension;

Decreases fibrin, reducing tendency toward blood clots;

Builds up additional blood supply routes in the heart.

To get the kind of benefits we've outlined above, two things must be kept firmly in mind. First of all, there is a world of difference between purposeful exercise and activity that just makes us tired. Lots of people say, "Oh I don't need an exercise program; I get lots of exercise in the course of my daily work — I'm on my feet all day." One woman said, "I'm a mother, isn't that enough?" Well, being a mother can be absolutely exhausting, but it doesn't necessarily follow that, along with the fatigue, being a mother provides the exercise that is required to keep the body healthy.

This leads us to the second factor. We do not exercise in order to get physically tired, we exercise in order to accomplish two very different objectives: (1) to stretch, extend, and use the muscles, tissues and organs in a manner that keeps them limber and healthy; and (2) to extend the aerobic capacities of the cardiovascular system.

Any program of exercise ought to include techniques that meet one or both of these needs. Both kinds are essential. It is not difficult to understand the purpose of bending, stretching, and lifting exercises, for we all know that muscles atrophy if they are not used. The purpose of aerobics is indicated by the name itself. *Aer* refers to "air" and an aerobic exercise is one devised to build up the intake of air. The result is an increase in the heartbeat and the burning of oxygen in the body. The goal of an aerobic exercise is to raise the heartbeat rate to a submaximal level. The formula used is 220 minus your age x 75%. During an aerobic exercise your heartbeat should approach but not surpass this figure.

So the most important question in selecting an aerobic exercise is not the specific activity — running, walking, playing tennis, playing golf, and so forth — but is it demanding enough to make aerobic demands upon your heart? Using this criteria, just plain strolling is not likely to be aerobically beneficial, but walking at a rate of four to five miles per hour is. Golf is rarely a good aerobic exercise (especially with a cart), unless it is very taxing (exasperating doesn't count). Badminton, volleyball, tennis doubles and even downhill skiing are usually *not* good aerobics (although if you play hard enough and continuously enough at these, they can be). Even squash and paddleball rate rather poorly.

So what is a good aerobic exercise? Tennis singles, if you are skilled and keep moving steadily for thirty minutes. Jogging or running at 5 miles per hour or better (although jogging is not universally good for everyone for other reasons). Cycling at 13 miles per hour or faster, continuous swimming, and probably best of all — cross-country skiing.

Now, before you start to smirk because none of the above appear to be within your range of possibilities, we need to tell you that calisthenics can be aerobically valuable if you pursue them in a rhythmic and continuous manner. We get our aerobics daily through running-in-place during our calisthenics and walking two-and-a-half to three miles at a brisk pace. So you can get aerobics without spending one cent for special equipment, clothing, or facilities.

Whenever possible, we like to use swimming and water exercise because it is so beneficial. For one thing, your weight in the water is about one tenth of what it is out of water. This means you can direct more energy to the part of the body being exercised—less is needed to hold you up. Swimming is excellent because it is easier for people with arthritis (the buoyancy of the water takes pressure off the limbs), people with lower back pains, those with injuries to the joints (who should not do jogging), heart patients, people who are overweight and those with varicose veins. Water exercise is particularly good for strengthening the muscles of the abdomen. The excess heat generated by your exercise is cooled by the water and your heart doesn't have to pump vertically against gravity. In addition there is an "isotonic" effect with the constant pressure of the water's flow and weight on the muscles. Swimming is also good for burning calories: a one hundred and fifty pound person swimming the crawl at 25–50 yards per minute can burn 750 calories per hour.

We have not included any exercises in this chapter because we believe that it is essential for you to select exercises that are most suitable to you. Just as it is a mistake not to extend yourself enough physically, so it is also a mistake to launch into a program that is too advanced for your own physical condition. And whatever exercises you do choose, make sure to do them at your own pace. We realize that's a kind of *carte blanche* for the person who is tempted to loaf through an exercise program. But if you want to loaf, then why exercise at all? It's your choice—you're in charge.[1]

Remember, the purpose of exercise is to maintain and improve what you have. Unlike some other resources, you do not use up what you have by exercise.

---

[1]See the end of this chapter for suggested resources, including some exercise programs.

Keep in mind that your body, unlike your car or your television, maintains its quality and fitness when you use it intelligently. Exercise, instead of using up longevity, actually prolongs it. The appliances in your home use up some of their expected "life" every time you flick a switch and turn them on. But your body wants to be used — not misused or abused — and thrives on it.

GAINING CONTROL THROUGH BIOFEEDBACK

We can hardly close our consideration of gaining control of the body without mentioning briefly biofeedback training. Having based this book on the premise that what you need is already within yourself, it may seem inappropriate to speak about biofeedback, inasmuch as it relies on some apparatus. But the apparatus simply aids you in learning to regulate some physical functions that are normally under the unconscious control of the autonomic nervous system. So biofeedback is not the technique, but merely a tool that helps you learn the techniques.

Biofeedback machines come in all sizes and shapes, and run from inexpensive to quite expensive. They may measure various biophysical responses in the body, but most of them to date have been designed to monitor and report four basic kinds of information:

- GSR (*galvanic skin response*): to measure the resistance of the skin to the passage of bodily electricity. High GSR indicates anxiety, tension.

- Skin temperature: to measure the flow of blood into the limbs. Controlling the temperature in the extremities assists in regulating some vascular problems, such as migraine headaches.

- EEG (*electroencephalogram*): to indicate the different kinds of brainwaves. Control of brainwaves enables subjects to induce certain states of consciousness.

- EMG (*electromyograph*): measuring the impulses generated by the muscles of the forehead. Control of these impulses aids in reduction of tension.

The GSR biofeedback machine we use is quite inexpensive and smaller than a pocket radio. By means of either an auditory signal or a visual gauge, we can hear or see when someone is in varying degrees of relaxation and tension. Because we know how it "feels" within when we are in those states, we have learned to relax (lowering the GSR reading) at will, and you, too, can learn how to do this. What we—and many others—have learned is self-regulation, which is control over certain physical responses, as well as control over states of mind that govern emotions. Barbara Brown says that "Medically, this is government by the consent of the governed." [2]

In chapter 3 we briefly mentioned autogenic training. Actually, autogenic training attempts pretty much the same thing as biofeedback training—self-regulation—but without any biofeedback equipment. The graduated exercises of autogenic training are dependent upon biofeedback—that is to say, information from your own body—but the feedback is in the form of your own personal feelings about what is happening, instead of signals generated through an auditory or visual device. As you might expect, autogenic training is therefore slower and more difficult than biofeedback training, but the results are pretty much the same.

We have already given you a version of the first autogenic training technique in chapter 3: the inducement of a feeling of "heaviness," and with it relaxation. Immediately following is

---

[2]Barbara B. Brown, Ph.D., *New Mind, New Body* (New York: Harper & Row, 1974), p. xiii.

the second autogenic training exercise, which usually takes considerably more practice than the first one.

To do this exercise, turn to page 41 and follow all the procedures for autogenic training exercise one, except that you substitute the words: "The fingers of my LEFT (right) hand are getting warm." In time, after practice, you should be able to feel a sensation of warmth in the fingers and direct it to spread to your hand and arm. (If you were using a biofeedback skin temperature probe, you could, of course, get feedback or information about the rise of temperature in your fingers from the temperature gauge.)

Elmer and Alyce Green (of the Menninger Clinic in Topeka, Kansas) have been pioneers in the use of both biofeedback and autogenic training in helping thousands of people to learn to self-regulate some of their physical functions for the purpose of curing various maladies or at least to alleviate symptoms. The Greens believe that we are just on the edge of a broad new field that will have tremendous impact on healing and expanding the capacities of mind, body, and spirit. We agree.

RESOURCES FOR FURTHER STUDY AND SELF-DEVELOPMENT

Brown, Barbara B. *Between Health & Illness*. Boston: Houghton Mifflin, 1984.

———. *New Mind, New Body*. New York: Harper & Row, 1974.

Cooper, Kenneth. *Aerobics*. New York: J.P. Lippincott, 1968.

Goldberg, Philip. *Executive Health*. New York: McGraw-Hill, 1978, Chapter 8.

Green, Elmer and Alyce. *Beyond Biofeedback*. New York: Dell, 1977.

McQuade, Walter and Aikman, Ann. *Stress.* New York: E.P. Dutton, 1974.

Pelletier, Kenneth R. *Longevity: Fulfilling Our Biological Potential.* New York: Delacorte, 1981, Chapter 7.

_____. *Mind as Healer—Mind as Slayer.* New York: Dell, 1977.

Shealy, C. Norman, M.D. *90 Days to Self-Health.* New York: Dial, 1977, Chapter 7.

Stein, Richard A., M.D. *Personal Strategies for Living With Less Stress.* New York: John Gallagher, 1983, Chapter 5.

*   *   *

A simple biofeedback machine is available from:

> Thought Technology, Ltd.
> 2180 Belgrave Avenue
> Montreal, Quebec
> Canada H4A2L8

The machine is the GSR/Temp 2. Write for a catalog of bio-feedback devices.

*   *   *

"Manage Your Stress" is the title of a four-cassette tape set by Dr. Ken Dychtwald and available from:

> The Soundworks, Inc.
> P.O. Box 10868
> Arlington, VA 22210.

CHAPTER

TO
SLEEP . . .

It was an evening very early in our marriage. As Larry settled into bed, Valere turned to him and said, "Now, let's talk about some of the repairs we have to do around the house. First, let's decide whether to go ahead and put on a new roof . . . "

"Hold on," said Larry in disbelief, "you've got to be kidding."

"About a new roof?" replied Valere with equal incredulity.

"No, no," Larry responded, "about discussing it now at bedtime."

"I thought that was a good time for pillow talk," Valere insisted.

"Well, it may be for you, but it's not for me. I'm not sure I know what pillow talk is, but anything as important as improvements to the house I prefer to do when I'm wide awake. But even more important, I found a long time ago that nothing is so likely to keep me awake as mulling over a problem in bed."

Although reluctantly at first, Valere acceded to Larry's ideas about not stimulating the mind unnecessarily at bedtime. The result: we both sleep better — better, it would seem, than lots of people with whom we consult.

It has been estimated that perhaps 40 percent of the people in the USA have trouble sleeping. (We're not talking about people who occasionally have trouble sleeping, but of those who find it a continuing, if not nightly, problem.) Sleeping problems seem to be manifested in three different ways: (1) difficulty in falling asleep; (2) waking up frequently during the night; and (3) difficulty in going back to sleep once awakened.

Obviously, many people experience two or even three of the above problems. We have experienced these problems, as well, although not always every night. From our own experience and reflection upon it, we made some important discoveries that have virtually eliminated our "sleep problems" as well as those of many people with whom we've counseled.

As with so many other things in life, we have discovered that the greatest cause of sleep problems is our understanding and attitude about sleep. Many people do not sleep well because they are anxious about not sleeping. Larry had learned well the high school health class maxim that eight hours of sleep per night is essential to good health. Holding fast to that magic number of "8," he became apprehensive whenever it seemed he was likely to be getting less than the prescribed number of hours. The more often he failed to get eight hours of sleep, the more anxious he became about his "sleep problem" and soon his anxiety about the problem was keeping him from falling asleep. On those nights of tossing and turning, he would periodically check the clock to see how much time he had already lost. His response to this information would be to frantically "try to go to sleep," lest he lose any more of that golden unconsciousness.

One day it occurred to him that it was his anxiety about sleeping, not his sleeplessness, that was exhausting him and he hit upon a maxim that, scientifically true or not, cured him of his sleep problems: I DO NOT NEED TO SLEEP; I NEED ONLY TO REST; WHEN MY BODY OR MIND NEEDS IT, SLEEP WILL COME.

The result was almost miraculous. No longer afraid of not sleeping, he went to bed with a different attitude. He would go to bed every night for approximately eight hours of rest. He would sleep only when his body/mind decided it was necessary. Freed of anxiety about sleeplessness, falling asleep was quite effortless. Many people fail to sleep because they exert an effort to do so. Our efforts to sleep are almost always futile and counterproductive. We do not *make* ourselves sleep; we *let* sleep happen.

The very first step in curing yourself of sleeplessness is to release that terrible anxiety that you are not going to sleep and that your lack of sleep is going to be injurious. That change in attitude alone might make all the difference in the world to you in your sleep habits. It has for both of us.

Since making that first discovery for ourselves, we have learned a great deal more about sleep and sleep problems. Much of this information has come from various sleep clinics that are helping people with serious sleep problems.

One of the first things we look for when people come to us with sleep problems is the accuracy of their perception of the problem. Is it really insomnia that they have? Many people suffer from what may be called pseudoinsomnia. Actually, they may not have insomnia at all, or it may not be nearly as serious as they think. The severity of the complaint may bear little relation to the amount of sleep they are actually lacking. Often they are suffering from anxiety, not insomnia.

For example, many people get enough sleep, but, because it is a shallow sleep with quite a bit of wakefulness involved, they interpret this as sleeplessness. What they do not realize is that a normal night of sleep involves a series of cycles of different levels of consciousness, and only a relatively short period of the night is devoted to what we regard as "deep sleep." In other words, "light sleep" is part of the normal pattern of sleep. It does not represent a failure to sleep. Most of these people are getting sufficient sleep, although they do not know it. Their judgment may be seriously affected by a time distortion — they think they've slept only a few minutes, when, in fact, they were asleep for an hour or more.

We also try to help people realize that the need for sleep varies greatly with individuals. We do not all need the same amount of sleep, just as we don't all need the same amount of food and oxygen. As our energy and metabolism levels vary from person to person, so does the need for sleep. Eight hours of sleep is an average, not a norm.

The time factor in sleep needs is tied to the personal body rhythm. Some people function well with eight hours of sleep followed by sixteen hours of wide-awake activity of consciousness. Other people seem to find just as beneficial what is called polyphasic sleep, a cycle or pattern of shorter sleep periods in bed, supplemented by one or more naps or light sleep. Instead of getting upset because you sleep considerably less than eight hours at night and then get drowsy at times during the day, you need simply to accept that your needs are different and adjust your daily schedule accordingly.

We have also learned that it's natural and normal for people to sleep less as they grow older. Your need for sleep diminishes as you age — a reality which, we realize, is quite contrary to popular expectation. In addition, as you grow older, it is normal for the number of awakenings per night to increase. This number normally increases gradually until the age of forty for men, seventy for women. After this, the increase in awakenings increases rapidly. If you awake more frequently during the night as you get older, you need to adjust to this reality as a normal aspect of aging, rather than viewing it as abnormal and becoming anxious about it.

Having considered all of the above, you may have concluded that your insomnia is real, not *pseudo*. What then? Sleeping pills? Our answer: only as a last resort when everything else has been proven ineffective, and then only as a very short-term measure.

It is estimated that in America alone, thirty million sleeping pills are consumed nightly. Sales of sleeping pills total over one million dollars annually, second only to aspirin. Many physicians realize the limitations and even dangers of sleeping pills and are very conservative in prescribing them. At the same time, from the people with whom we've counseled, it would appear that many physicians prescribe them indiscriminately and even irresponsibly. Some people we know have been taking sleeping pills nightly for years. Because they are a prescription drug, that kind of usage can only be assumed to be accomplished with the assistance of a physician, a kind of professional "junkie."

If that seems a harsh judgment, consider the relevant facts about sleeping pills. Many have dangerous side effects resulting from the antihistamines, bromides, and scopolamine these pills contain. Among these side effects are problems with the kidneys, liver, circulatory and respiratory systems, hypertension, problems of the central nervous system, digestive tract, as well as emotional and behavioral disorders.

Furthermore there is the problem of addiction. Once dependent upon sleeping pills — whether the dependence is real or imagined — many people find they are unable to experience normal pill-free sleep. Sleeping pills tend to lose their effectiveness within the first two weeks of regular usage. Thereafter there is a steady decline in the efficacy of the pill. The user often responds with increased usage. The body's tolerance for the pill increases rapidly. It is also said that addiction to sleeping pills is as hard to break as a heroin habit.

Probably the worst characteristic of sleeping pills is that they disturb the normal sleep patterns. What you get from sleeping pills is not a natural sleep, but a *narcosis* — a depression of the central nervous system by means of interfering with the passage of impulses to the brain. Sleeping pills deliver what one writer described as a "knock-out blow to the brain cells." The effect is a paralysis of the nerve cells.

Another harmful effect of sleeping pills is the disturbance of the normal pattern of the REM (rapid-eye-movement) state of sleep. The REM state is part of the normal sleep cycle which occurs four to seven times per night, and is the state in which most dreaming takes place. Deprivation of REM sleep has been demonstrated in the laboratory to result in impaired capacity for learning, memory loss, and other psychological disturbances. Although sleeping pills will render you unconscious, what you are getting is not a restful sleep and, over a period of time, the loss of your natural sleep pattern will affect you physically and quite possibly psychologically. Although we would not say that you should never resort to sleeping pills, we have no hesitation in advising you to make them a matter of last and brief resort. And if you never use sleeping pills, please know that you will not have missed anything of much value.

So, how can we cure sleeplessness without resorting to pills and alcohol? (Incidentally, although alcohol may induce unconsciousness, it is also destructive to normal sleep patterns.) We believe that usually the answer to sleep problems can be found within. For most people, we have found, sleeplessness is a learned habit, frequently representing an inadequate response to stress.

Sometimes disturbing factors exist that are external rather than internal (although, to be accurate, they are still dependent upon your internal reaction to the external stimulus). So, before you go looking within, let's first take a look at the external factors that could contribute or be responsible for your sleep problem:

• *Physical aches or pains.* Sometimes your body may be so uncomfortable that your attention is held by your discomfort, and you are unable to fall asleep, or you may be awakened even after you have initially fallen asleep. When this is true, you will need to do whatever can be done to remove or make more compatible the discomfort.

- *Uncomfortable bed.* You can't get a good night's rest if your bed is just plain uncomfortable, sometimes even downright painful. Your bed may be too hard, too soft, too short, too lumpy, or something else that causes you discomfort. Sometimes this discomfort is so subtle that you hardly notice it. Most of us will buy deluxe automobiles, luxurious furniture, and "cheap-out" on the one item in which you spend the greatest part of every day. So, before you begin a probe of your psyche, check your bed—particularly the mattress and springs. You may not have to look further.

- *Unfavorable environmental conditions.* Temperature and noise are two of the most frequent culprits in robbing you of sleep. Even if they are not the sole cause of sleeplessness, they will often contribute substantially to your bad sleep habit. Once again, noise and temperature may be factors of which you are either unaware or just barely aware. You may be awakened during the night without quite realizing that it was a faint sound of a train whistle, or a gradual change in temperature or humidity that roused you from your slumber. Sometimes the problem may be an odor that calls you back from your sleep.

    Having acknowledged the role that these phenomena may play in disturbing your sleep, it is also necessary to point out that noise, temperature, and odors by themselves do not have the power to disturb your sleep, but only your sensitivity to them. If you ever moved to a new location where the noise pattern was quite different than that to which you were accustomed, perhaps you noticed that in time you unconsciously adjusted to the noises. When you fail to sleep through various noises, you may have already decided that those noises will disturb you. Once again, although you may not be able to do much to change the noise level, you can-

change the way you will respond to it. This can also be true
with temperature, odors, and other physical factors.

- *"Togetherness."* Do you have difficulty sleeping when you share
  the bed, or even just the room, with someone else? This may
  happen because the other person makes sleep noises, or
  because he or she is a restless or light sleeper with sleep
  problems of his or her own. Sometimes there is nothing to be
  done but to get your own bed or own room — providing that is
  possible. But the other obvious solution is to learn to be less
  sensitive to the disturbances. Of course, it is obvious that if
  your roommate snores like a freight train on a rough track,
  this may be asking a great deal of your inner resources (perhaps, even, too much).

These are some of the physical factors that may cause or
contribute to sleep problems. If you can do anything about
them, by all means do all you can. If you can't, or if making
these changes is financially prohibitive, the answer may well be
in making an inner adjustment to the externals.

Let's take a look at some of the psychological reasons for
sleep problems. These are often even less apparent than the
external factors. Usually they relate to some inner attitude
which may be hidden in your unconscious. Sleeplessness is
frequently the result of an *unconscious resistance to sleep or sleeping.*
Often it is a carry-over from childhood, when sleep represented
a lack of autonomy. As a child, you may have tried various
strategies for avoiding sleep as a way of asserting your independence. Sometimes, particularly with people whose problems of
autonomy are carried into the adult years, these resistances are
maintained long past the years of childhood. Going to bed may
still represent "giving in" to an authority outside yourself. Similar to this childish resistance is the association of the bedroom
as *the place of punishment.* "Go to your room!" is long-remem-
bered in the unconscious, long after it is forgotten in the con-

scious mind. So, some of you may resist sleep because the bedroom still is remembered as a place of banishment.

If after some earnest searching of your psyche, you conclude that your sleep problems may be either caused or accentuated by a lingering childish resistance, you can change your unconscious aversion to sleep by making a conscious effort to think of sleep and the bedroom in a positive, constructive light.

Another psychological reason for avoiding sleep is a largely unconscious fear of death. Some people associate loss of consciousness with a final oblivion. To close your eyes in sleep suggests a possibly permanent loss of contact with the physical world. It would seem logical to conclude that, since you have obviously fallen asleep and wakened safely and alive in the morning many, many times, you should no longer associate sleep with death. But there is nothing that says the unconscious needs to be logical. So, when the fear of death keeps you from sleep, you need to tackle it consciously. By changing your inner feelings about death, you can also change the way you react to it.

Sometimes you may have sleep problems because you're afraid of dreams and nightmares. Because you may have had some frightening experiences with dreams in the past, you unconsciously fight sleep in apprehension that you will have to go through similarly terrifying experiences again. In the next chapter you will learn how to work with your dreams so that you need not ever again fear them.

Or, you might resist sleep because you are reluctant to let go of one or more of your problems. Just as in chapter 1 we saw that some people worry because, in a perverse way, they "enjoy" their problems, so some people don't want to let go of a troubling situation even to sleep. To let go of your problems so you can sleep will mean you have to make an inner adjustment in how you handle these situations. Once you accept that you don't have to "worry them to death" and that worrying about-them doesn't do anything to help you solve them, you can learn to let go long enough to get some sleep.

HOW CAN WE TREAT SLEEP PROBLEMS WITHOUT DRUGS?

In order to take care of your own sleep problems, first, take an inventory of both external and internal factors: Why can't I sleep? Having determined one or more reasons for your problem, consider possible ways of meeting the problem(s). For example you could check any possible dietary factors: are you deficient in calcium and/or vitamin B? Are your sleep problems ever caused by overeating and/or overdrinking? When the digestive system has to labor too hard to digest a late and/or heavy meal, it may substantially impair your ability to sleep. Is your intake of caffeine disruptive to sleep? Keep in mind caffeine is found not only in coffee and tea, but also chocolate, cola, and some pain pills such as Anacin and Excedrin.

You can use imagery to put you in the right frame of mind for sleeping, especially by visualizing peaceful, serene surroundings and situations. (See chapter 9 for assistance with imagery techniques.) Relaxation techniques will also help you prepare your body and mind for sleep. (See chapter 3 for specific techniques.) And, you can use meditation to gain mastery over your mind, allowing the unconscious to take charge over you in sleep. (See chapter 8.)

Exercise will prepare your body for sleep. Just as exercise helps your body to physically relax, so it can be a valuable aid in preparing your body for sleep. It might seem that exercise would tend to stimulate you, but, actually, it can have the opposite effect. Please remember that, while physical fatigue may interfere with sleep, a carefully-planned program of regular exercise will be sleep-enhancing.

Regulate your sensory and mental input. One of the easiest ways to keep your mind from dwelling on problems and concerns at bedtime is to fill it with something else. A sure-fire method is reading, particularly if the reading material is not too stimulating. The harder it is for you to get to sleep, the less stimulating your reading material should be. You may need to select something quite dull, even boring. We have a whole filing cabinet of old sermons that should do the trick for just about anyone!

If negative thoughts can keep you awake, positive thoughts can often help you sleep. When Larry was a seminary student, he had a classmate who was frequently the butt of good-natured humor because he was found fast asleep on his knees beside his bed several times. "If your prayers are that boring to you, just think how they must affect the Lord!" his classmates would chide. But we have since found that Larry's sleepy classmate may have discovered something. Falling asleep at prayer is probably no offense to God, and it is frequently a good means of entering the state of sleep in a peaceful, contented manner. Perhaps you may remember that popular song of quite a few seasons ago:

When I'm worried,
And I can't sleep,
I count my blessings,
Instead of sheep,
And I fall asleep
Counting my blessings.

Try it. It works.

RESOURCES FOR FURTHER STUDY AND SELF-DEVELOPMENT

Goldberg, Philip. *Executive Health.* New York: McGraw-Hill, 1977, Chapter 9.

Hauri, Peter, Ph.D. *Sleep Well With Biofeedback.* Montreal: Thought Technology Ltd. (Audio cassette and workbook.)

LeCron, Leslie M. *Self Hypnotism.* New York: Prentice Hall, 1964, Chapter 11.

CHAPTER

TAKE CHARGE
OF YOUR
MIND

Fifteen minutes a day that can change your life! That's what meditation can do. And we guarantee it will work! You don't get many offers like that today, do you? "Guaranteed?" Yes, we can guarantee that meditation will work for you. It can change you—mind, body and spirit. The only reason we say "can" change you instead of "will" change you, is that we can guarantee what meditation will do, but we cannot guarantee what you will do. And you, as always, are the most important factor in the equation.

You may remember the story of the rich young ruler who came to Jesus asking how to obtain eternal life. He indicated he would do anything, but when Jesus told him what to do, we are told that instead "he went away sorrowed for he had great possessions" (Mark 10:17–22). His possessions—the very thing Jesus said he would need to give up—were really more important than the eternal life he thought was his heart's desire.

Christ's "method" was guaranteed; what he could not guarantee, however, was the young man's response.

We have found that there are lots of people who get interested in meditation because they want to change their lives in some way—mind, body or spirit. But, having taught them the techniques, we often find that they go away like the rich young ruler, "sorrowed" because the fifteen minutes per day meditation required was more than they wanted to spend on changing their lives.

In chapter 4 we told you that Larry's "arthritis" went away after he began a concentrated daily program of relaxation, meditation, and imagery. He began meditating because he wanted relief from the aches and pains. But, like most practitioners of meditation, he got much more than he had been seeking.

When Larry began meditating, he used the relaxation technique outlined in chapter 3, along with several meditative modes. He experienced a reduction in the rate of his respiration, a marked reduction in GSR (resistance of skin to electrical impulses and a measure of anxiety), a reduction in the rate of heartbeat, oxygen consumption, cardiac output, concentration of blood lactate (another indication of anxiety), and a change of EEG brainwaves to a level that are the direct opposite of those that indicate anxiety. All of this brought him a state of relaxation, physical renewal, and control over his body that alone seemed to justify the fifteen minutes per day it required. And there is nothing unusual in the physical results he experienced in meditation—just about everyone does.

Along with the physical benefits, meditation also helps you to take charge of your mind. One of the universal benefits of meditation is the improvement in your power of concentration, that ability to focus your mind on a task and gain access to a greater range of internal resources in accomplishing that task. It can enable you to work better in the midst of distractions, to desensitize yourself to annoyances that are sometimes beyond your control.

Meditation is also invaluable in helping you to work better with your emotions, particularly the negative, destructive ones. It is impossible to sustain anger, anxiety, and resentment when you are in the midst of a meditative state. And, dissipating destructive emotions through meditation does not mean you are sweeping them under the rug, or burying them in the unconscious where they continue to stress you, or literally and figuratively "eat away at you." Thus meditation is a very important means of dealing with the major stressors of life.

Meditation is also invaluable, we have found, in releasing creativity, developing your power of intuition, and preparing to give or receive healing, as we will indicate in chapters 9 through 11. For us, as well as for countless others, meditation has also been a means of communion with God—an aid and supplement to prayer.

Meditation is hard to define, and the more we experience and the more we learn, the more we have come to realize that meditation cannot be categorized neatly. No one can rightly say, "*This* is meditation and nothing else is."

Some meditation teachers have acknowledged that meditation is a lot like "progressive relaxation." Others have noticed the similarities with what is often called "creative imagination" or "imagery." Some Christian writers—Morton Kelsey for one—claim that the historic Christian discipline of contemplation is a type of meditation. Other people have wondered whether meditation, as we teach it, is not really hypnosis, or at least self-hypnosis. While we maintain that meditation and hypnosis are not really the same, it is true that both are dependent upon the suggestability of the mind. Meditation is all this—and more. Don't let anyone try to put it in a nice, neat little package for you. What matters is not what you call it, or how you do it, but that you do it regularly and devotedly.

Regardless of what or who brings you to meditate, you will find in meditating that you gain access to a part of yourself that, except in dreams (or in flashes of intuition, creativity, or transcendental experiences) is largely hidden from your aware-

ness. You know there is something in you called the unconscious, but most people have little idea what that's all about.
Strangely enough, our society's beginning to realize that it is
the unconscious that is really the larger part of our being.
Freud and Jung have depicted the self as very much like an
iceberg: the small part showing above the water represents the
conscious mind, and the physical world of sense experience,
time, and space; the much, much larger portion under the
waterline being unconscious, the nonmaterial, the spiritual
world, where memories are hidden, behavior is motivated,
autonomic bodily functions are governed, creativity lies waiting, dreams are generated, where we discover the true Self
and, many would add — we among them — the God-within-us
resides.

Just because you may be largely unaware of this other part
of you doesn't mean that it is not important. Many people are
learning today what religious teachers and philosophers have
been teaching for centuries. As Morton Kelsey says, "A human
being is bigger than just rational consciousness."[1] If you are to
know the fullness in which you were created, you need to both
be aware of this "other self" and be in communication or even
communion with it. Just as society is realizing that full human
potential is achieved only when the left and right side of the
brain are in some kind of harmony, so you need to find ways
and means of bringing the conscious and unconscious into that
same kind of relationship. You cannot afford to shut yourself
off from the depth of your own being. When you are in touch
with it, says Kelsey, then you have the "single eye" that makes
you whole.

Let's look at a negative illustration of this idea. In a certain
town, the local bank president (who is also chairman of the
United Fund and Sunday school superintendent of the local

---

[1]Morton Kelsey, *The Other Side of Silence, A Guide to Christian Meditation* (New
York: Paulist Press, 1976), p. 158.

Protestant church) goes on a sudden rampage and, appearing suddenly in the town square, shoots and kills fifteen people before he is finally gunned down by police. The townspeople cannot believe it is the same man they knew. "The kindest, most considerate man I ever knew," says one disbelieving neighbor. "He was always the mediator in any dispute," protests another. "This is not the father and husband we know," wails his family. "What happened?" everyone wants to know.

This is a fictitious example, but not at all unlike some of the things you read in your daily newspaper. Frequently, it is found in examining these people over a period of time, that they have suffered from a "split personality," to use an oversimplified term. The Jekyll/Hyde phenomenon indicates a conscious and unconscious that are seriously in conflict, often, it would seem, in almost complete ignorance of one another.

This is obviously an extreme example, but we chose it because it helps you understand in dramatic terms what may exist in each of you quite subtly—not that you have a Mr. Hyde hidden within the depths of your being, but that there is probably more to who you are than you know. Nor do we want to suggest that that part of yourself which is hidden from you is necessarily evil; it is probably some of both. We are just trying to make a case for there being more of the "real you" than you probably know.

Sometimes some of that "real you" comes to the surface in moments of emergency, challenge, inspiration, creativity, and in dreams, as we'll explore in chapter 8. Meditation is another means of access into the unconscious and the other self. Morton Kelsey calls it "the art of letting down the barrier that separates one's rational consciousness from the depth of one's soul."[2] Others would call it the means of entering one or more higher states of consciousness.

---

[2]Kelsey, *Other Side of Silence,* p. 37.

We have previously mentioned the use of the electroen-
cephalograph for the measurement of brain waves in different
states of consciousness. If an EEG reading were made of your
brain waves at this moment, we hope they would be between
14 and 22 pulses per second. This is the *beta* state, the state of
consciousness in which you are wide-awake and conscious of
what is outside your own mind. If you are really into this
chapter, you might even be in the *alpha* state, 8 to 13 cycles per
second, indicating a state of intense concentration that is not
very susceptible to distraction.

But perhaps what you've been reading here has triggered
some deeper more intense thinking, so that momentarily you
are so intent upon your thoughts that you are oblivious to what
is happening around you. This is the *theta* state, a state of
creativity with the brain cycles down to 4 to 7 per second.
(People in hypnotic states are likely to be in *theta*.) Maybe,
however, you found this all very dull and your brain waves
have decreased to 1 to 3 per second. This is *delta,* but you are
not aware of it, because you are now asleep!

Only when we are in the *beta* state are we susceptible to
anxiety and distress. For example, if you are asleep and your
smoke alarm wakes you, it has jolted your consciousness from a
delta to a *beta* state. In meditation, the direction is just the
opposite — meditation is a journey inward to either the *alpha* or
theta state. The *alpha* state of intense concentration is very beneficial, but it is in the deeper *theta* and *delta* states that you find
your greatest access to the unconscious.

Meditation, therefore, is a life-changing discipline that
can be used for any of the following reasons or combination
thereof:

> to explore or commune with your own unconscious;
> to gain control over your own mind;
> to gain control over your own body;
> to encounter the God-within-you.

We have experienced success in all four of these categories and you can, too.

The meditative state is sometimes described as "passive alertness." This may come as a surprise if you associate meditation with a form of drowsiness. Instead, the mind in meditation is very alert, while the body is relaxed. But "alertness" does not mean activity. In fact, the task in meditation is to shut down the activity of your mind in its aggressive search for data, and achieve a state of quietude in which it can be fully alert, aware, and responding to a much greater depth of sensitivity. Meditation is more a state of knowing than of thinking. The key difference is that in meditation you *let* the mind become alert; you do not *make* it alert. Instead of propelling yourself toward something, in meditation you permit yourself to be drawn to it or let it come to you.

Another key to meditation is concentration, a term which seems more aggressive than passive. You may think you have to "try" to concentrate, but in meditation you "let" yourself concentrate. Emptying the mind so you can concentrate is not like trying to pick lint off a flannel suit. Remember, we said you cannot get rid of a negative with another negative? So, in meditation you empty the mind, not by trying to get rid of the bits and pieces that are there, but by filling the mind with something that leaves no room for the bits and pieces.

That doesn't mean you will not have distractions. In fact, you will probably experience more distractions than you ever dreamed existed. It is when you are meditating that you will hear sounds to which previously you have been oblivious—the creaking of floor boards, the hum of electricity in the wall clock, an airplane flying overhead, the symphony of your own internal organs! You will also become aware of other sense distractions. Your ear will itch, your toe will throb, your body hair will move ever so slightly, causing you to flick at non-existent bugs! And at the same time, you will find your mind finally compiling the grocery list it has avoided all day. That's all par for the course. There are vested interests in your being that will struggle to keep you from opening the door into the unconscious. The conscious mind will kick and scream to hang on to your attention.

In meditation, however, you do not *fight* your distractions—that would only make them stronger. Instead, passively let go of them. When they float into the view of your mind's eye, don't zap them with a mental laser beam. Don't indignantly tell them to "get lost." In fact, don't have any feelings about them at all. Let them float by and out of your attention. Even if they have grabbed hold of your attention, don't let them hold on to it. *Let go.*

There is one other thing we must tell you before we turn you loose into meditation: never, never be critical of your performance in meditation, and do not evaluate your experience. This is one activity in which it is the process, not what you *feel* the results to be that is important. There will be a cumulative effect that is often hidden from you. There will be days when your meditation will leave you "feeling good" and other days when you will say, "Nothing happened." But neither of these subjective reactions are the true measure of what will happen to you while you meditate. It is over the long run that you will be able to experience the benefits.

There has been a great deal of research data on the beneficial effects of meditation, but we will cite only two to give you an idea. One of these was a study by Dr. David Frew in which 500 people using Transcendental Meditation were interviewed. Among the long-term benefits reported were increased job satisfaction, improved job performance, reduction in turnover potential, and improved relationships on the job.[3] Another study was reported by Jay Marcus in *TM And Business* (McGraw-Hill, 1978). This is what the 36 executives studied had to say:

---

[3]Philip Goldberg, *Executive Health,* (New York: McGraw-Hill, 1978), p. 213.

37% needed less sleep;
50% fell asleep faster;
37% used less hard liquor;
23% used less wine and beer;
55% eliminated or reduced cigarettes;
20% used less aspirin;
20% used less coffee;
53% felt more confident;
60% had more emotional stability;
53% improved their ability to organize.[4]

Note that in both studies one of the claimed results was improved performance. This has also been our personal experience: whatever we do, we tend to do it better and with less effort if we meditate. The fifteen minutes we devote to meditation each day is not really a *subtraction* from our available time, but an *addition* to it. Let no one alibi that they don't have time for meditation — you don't have time NOT to meditate!

HOW CAN WE LEARN TO MEDITATE?

There are many ways to meditate. We'll discuss just a few them. When you have mastered them, you may move on to more advanced techniques with guidance from other books and teachers. The most important thing is perseverance. Don't plan to meditate once or twice just to see what happens. You learn to meditate the way you learn to play a musical instrument — practice, practice, practice.

Begin with the relaxation technique outlined in chapter 3. Relaxation is the prelude to meditation. Of course, when you are beginning meditation, you'll need to go through the relaxa-

---

[4]Goldberg, *Executive Health,* p. 214.

tion procedure step-by-step. But in time you may find that you can eliminate parts of the relaxation procedure because you have learned to let go of your physical body by simply telling it to relax. Often, all you have to do is the very first part, saying to yourself: *"Relax . . . Relax . . . Relax . . . "* Other times, when you are more tense, you may have to go through the whole procedure or a portion of it. You will learn to judge just how much of the routine you need.

Don't attempt to begin meditation until you have entered a relaxed state. Of course, the relaxation technique will have already narrowed your field of attention and begun to concentrate your mind. There are two major approaches to meditation: (1) the guided meditation in which you are guided through a specific itinerary, and (2) the open meditation, when you allow yourself to be led without an itinerary.

GUIDED MEDITATIONS

Guided meditations are easier for beginners. You may want to record the instructions for the guided meditations on a tape cassette. If not, you will need to memorize the various steps inasmuch as your eyes need to be closed during the meditation.

The Rose Garden

Much more than you probably realize, the answers and resources you need for consciously meeting your challenges and concerns are within you. You may actually know the answer, but not be aware that you know. What you may need from your own mind may, for various reasons, be locked in. The "Rose Garden" is a guided meditation that will help you to tap the creative and therapeutic images in your own unconscious mind. Although you will probably find it helpful even on your first try, you will likely discover that your results will improve considerably with practice.

First, prepare yourself with a relaxation technique, including concentration on your breathing.

In your mind's eye, see and feel yourself standing in a beautiful meadow. Feel the warmth of the sun on your face; smell the freshness of the cool breeze; hear the sound of birds singing.

Then, look across the meadow to a beautiful forest and walk toward it. As you come closer, you see there is a path that leads into and through the forest.

As you enter the forest, you are struck by the remarkable sense of serenity and quiet you find there. Walking through the forest, you feel that serenity becoming a part of you.

Ahead, you see light at the end of the forest trail, and as you approach the light, you see that it leads you into a large clearing.

In the center of the clearing there is a large brick wall with a great wooden gate.

Walk up to the gate.

In your hand is a large metal key to the gate. You put it in the lock, turn it to the right and feel the large tumblers click as the bolt slides back.

You open the gate and walk inside, there beholding the most beautiful rose garden you have ever seen—row upon row of gorgeous roses in every imaginable color: red, white, yellow, pink, black, even orange and purple.

First, you will need to decide which color rose is your color. Take a second and make that decision.

Now, walk toward the row of roses that are the color you just selected. Walk down that row of roses, knowing that one of them is your rose, and your rose alone.

Finally, you stop, because you have found your rose and now you look at it in all its beauty.

Study its lines, contemplate its color, smell its fragrance.

Then, with your mind, gently bend back each of the rose petals, knowing that when you have reached the center of your flower, there will be in it a picture, symbol, or word(s) that has a special meaning for you alone.

At last, you lift back gently the last petal and you see the treasure it holds for you. Look at your treasure. You may immediately comprehend its meaning or you may not. Study it, taking in all its detail, allowing all its meaning to speak to you.

Then touch the rose and your treasure gently to your forehead, as if to absorb it.

Having taken it into your mind, let go of the rose and prepare to leave it, knowing you are taking with you your treasure.

Walk back along your row until you have left it behind and turn toward the gate. Take one last look at the rose garden as you prepare to exit the gate.

As you close the gate behind you, you turn the key in the lock to the left and hear the heavy bolt slide into place once more.

Now start back toward the path through the forest, entering it once more and walking in the peaceful quiet of it toward the green meadow.

When you emerge from the forest, you enter once again the bright sunshine and prepare to return to your normal state of consciousness.

Count to three as you open your eyes and resume that state of consciousness.

Note: You may use your "treasure" from the rose garden as a subject for future contemplation, if you like. For example, if the "gift" you find in your rose is a six-pointed Star of David, you might make it the focus of your meditation for several days or weeks until you feel that you have paid sufficient attention to it. If, during the meditation, you get an image you do not like, don't become anxious or resistant. Passively let the image fade. You do not have to accept anything negative if you don't want it.

The Meditation of the Bubble

This is also a structured meditation, an observation of your own stream of consciousness. The Bubble Meditation also allows you to get in touch with your unconscious mind, permitting you to time your concentration on each thought or perception and deal with it in a structured way. It also permits you to look at each thought individually without having to associate or connect it to another one — although that is o.k., if it happens. Remember, these "bubbles" are parts of you of which you are normally unaware.

In your mind's eye, see yourself sitting comfortably and peacefully on the bottom of a clear lake.

Each thought you will have during this meditation will be seen as a bubble that rises up through the water to the surface above. Each bubble, beginning from your mind, will take seven or eight seconds to reach the surface and disappear.

During the meditation, whenever you have a thought, image or perception, watch it as a bubble floating gently to the surface and then releasing it as it disappears.

You do not think *about* the bubble or the thought or try to associate with anything. You simply and passively observe it.

It is as if you are saying to yourself, "Oh, so that's what I'm thinking! How interesting."

Then, you calmly wait for the next bubble.

Don't be surprised or troubled if the same bubble rises several times. If you adopt a passive attitude, it will soon pass.

Do not be concerned if your mind goes blank, for blankness is also a bubble that you can observe.

The Breath Counting Meditation

This is also a structured meditation and its purpose is to help you do just one thing and one thing alone. You give all your attention to this simple task. In doing so you narrowly focus your attention, thereby driving competing thoughts and sensations out of your mind. The technique is to count as you exhale. Although Zen Masters usually count to ten, it is best for beginners to count only to four. Each time you reach "four," of course, you return to "one." After you have prepared yourself through relaxation and breathing, you proceed as follows:

Focus all your attention on breathing. Breath in, and as you exhale, silently count "one." Do the counting as passively as possible — never forcefully.

Inhale again, and then as you exhale, count "two." As you count, don't think about what you are thinking. It is as if you are observing yourself as you do it.

Breathe in again, and as you exhale, count "three."

Breathe in again, and breathing out count "four."

Inhale, and in exhaling, start once again at "one." And so on.

A Scriptural Meditation

Choose a narrative portion of scripture that is suitable for a deeper experience: the Feeding of the Five Thousand (Matthew 14:13–21), the Nativity of Jesus (Luke 2:1–20), the Wedding at Cana (John 2:1–11), the Stilling of the Wind and Sea

(Mark 4:35–41), and so forth. For the purpose of demonstration, we have chosen the Healing of a Paralytic in Luke 5:17–26. First, read the passage in your Bible. Having read it, go over it in your mind until you can recall all the details in sequence. Then, having prepared yourself through relaxation and deep breathing, imagine in your mind's eye the following:

You see yourself in this very same village of Galilee. Experience it with all five senses, letting your imagination supply each of these experiences.

See the house into which Jesus and his disciples have gone, as well as the tremendous group of people that have crowded into it, filling the doors and windows, so that no other person can get inside to be with the Master.

Note that this is a typical Palestinian house: along the side of the low building is a stairway that leads to the roof.

Now see a group of three men coming down the street, carrying a bed on which is lying a paralytic. Obviously, they want to bring him to Jesus, but there is no way to get into the house.

Seeing that they need help, you grasp one of the corners of the bed and motion with your head for them to carry the paralytic up the stairs to the roof. When you reach the roof of the house, you see that there are some loose tiles in the ceiling and you and your associates begin to lift these tiles out, one by one until there is a large space in the roof of the house.

Then, using some stout ropes, you and the other men begin to lower the paralytic on his bed through the opening in the roof. As you do, you see Jesus standing in the midst of the room. He does not seem particularly surprised at your "sanctified housebreaking," but looks at the paralytic with compassion.

Then glancing at the faces of your associates and yourself, you hear him say, "Man, your sins are forgiven you."

You watch intently to see what the paralytic will do. Cautiously, gradually, he sits up.

Immediately scribes and pharisees begin to question what Jesus has said. "Who is this that speaks blasphemies? Who can forgive sins but God only?"

With a patience you are afraid you could not muster, Jesus turns to them and says quietly, "Why do you question in your hearts? Which is easier, to say, 'Your sins are forgiven you,' or to say, 'Rise and walk'? But that you may know that the Son of man has authority on earth to forgive sins," and he turns to the paralytic and says: "I say to you, rise, take up your bed and go home."

The paralytic looks at Jesus, drops his feet over the side of the bed and slowly stands up. Then, cautiously, he puts one foot in front of the other and. . . . begins to walk! Delight comes into his eyes as he realizes he is healed. The crowd gasps in astonishment and you and your associates are overjoyed.

You hear a few people say, "Praise God," and "Thank you, Lord." And you find yourself silently thanking God.

Before you leave this place, there may be some friends whom you might also want to bring before the Master for healing. If so, picture each one being lowered through the roof into Jesus' presence.

When, at last you are ready to end the meditation, the crowd disperses slowly and you leave the house through the front door.

A Mantra Meditation

This is an ancient form of meditation that has been popularized by Transcendental Meditation. The basis of this technique is quite simple: a word or brief phrase is repeated over and over again, either aloud as a chant, or silently. It is your choice whether to do it audibly or not. So first choose your Mantra. It is best to choose a word or phrase that is not provocative. The idea of Mantra meditation is not to think about the Mantra, but to let the Mantra lead you to a state of detachment. You may choose God, Alleluia, Christ is Risen, Shalom, Oum (a universal Mantra for chanting), or, as Dr. Herbert Benson discovered, just the word "one." Peace, Love, Joy, Lord, Shanti are other possibilities.

The essence and program of Mantra meditation is simply to chant over and over again. No matter how often you find yourself straying from the task, always bring yourself gently back to it. Never reprove yourself for entertaining other thoughts or straying. But, as soon as you find yourself straying, bring yourself back. The rhythm of the chant is something best determined by yourself. Your task is to chant and to be aware only of your chanting.

RESOURCES FOR FURTHER STUDY AND SELF-DEVELOPMENT

Benson, Herbert, M.D. *The Relaxation Response.* New York: William Morrow, 1975.

Brooke, Avery. *How To Meditate Without Leaving The World.* Noroton, CT: Vineyard, 1975.

Ebon, Martin. *How To Find Peace of Mind Through Meditation.* New York: Signet, 1976.

Happold, F.C. *Prayer and Meditation: Their Nature and Practice.* Baltimore: Penguin, 1971.

Helleberg, Marilyn Morgan. *Beyond TM: A Practical Guide To The Lost Traditions of Christian Meditation.* New York: Paulist Press, 1980.

Kelsey, Morton T. *The Other Side of Silence: A Guide to Christian Meditation.* New York: Paulist Press, 1976 (An excellent book on *why* meditate.)

Leshan, Lawrence. *How to Meditate.* New York: Little Brown, 1974 (The single best book on *how* to meditate.)

Pelletier, Kenneth R. *Mind As Healer — Mind As Slayer.* New York: Dell, 1977, Chapter 6.

_____. *Toward a Science of Consciousness.* New York: Dell, 1978, Chapter 5.

Pipkin, H. Wayne. *Christian Meditation: Its Art and Practice.* New York: Hawthorne, 1977.

Smith, Bradford. *Meditation.* New York: Lippincott, 1963.

Tyson, Richard, M.D. with Walker, Jay R. *The Meditation Diet.* Chicago: Playboy Press, 1976.

White, John. *Everything You Want to Know About TM — Including How to Do It.* New York: Pocket Books, 1976.

*   *   *

"How To Relax and Meditate," a cassette tape by Larry Althouse, available through the New Dimensions Center, First United Methodist Church, Ross and Harwood Streets, Dallas, TX 75201. Write for prices.

CHAPTER

PERCHANCE
TO
DREAM

In 1950 Valere was enrolled in a psychology course at Southern Methodist University. The class was instructed to come to the next few sessions with several recent recorded dreams. Valere found that a bit unnerving because she almost never remembered her dreams; in fact, she really didn't dream all that often.

Several class sessions and nights went by without any dreams to record. Fortunately, the course instructor had not yet called on her. But, at last he did and she had to confess that she had no dreams to report. "Make sure you have some tomorrow," he warned her.

But "tomorrow" and "tomorrow" and "tomorrow" came and still she had no dreams to report, even though each night before going to sleep she gritted her teeth and told herself to "get busy and dream."

"Either you come with some dreams tomorrow," said the instructor, "or you're out."

She was desperate: she needed these course credits and it was already too late to transfer to another course. So, that night as she prepared to go to sleep, she prayed earnestly: "Dear God, please, please give me at least one dream to remember." The next morning when she awoke, despair settled over her because she didn't remember having dreamed during the night. But, as she began to get out of bed, her eyes fell on the notebook she had placed on her night table. There she found sixteen pages of dreams which she had evidently recorded during the night and then forgotten.

She was baffled, but also very thankful, and rushed off to class with her recorded dreams, presenting them to the instructor with a sigh of relief. He took a while to read the dreams before looking up and announcing, "These were worth waiting for. In fact, this is marvelous: you've managed in one night to cover all of Jung's archetypes in your dreams."

Those were Valere's first recorded dreams — almost her first remembered dreams — but she has been remembering and recording her dreams ever since. This she has continued to do, not out of idle curiosity, but because she has learned what the ancients knew and humanity has had to relearn again and again: dreams are an important means of communication with the inner self in that non-material realm wherein we may often also encounter God.

Upon making a survey of biblical literature, both Old and New Testaments, Larry discovered that dreams were one of the main channels of revelation from God to individuals in the Bible. Often, it seemed, God spoke to people in their dreams because this is when they were most open to his message. There are sixty-five passages in the Old Testament alone that deal with dreams specifically. Often, the writers of the Old Testament did not distinguish between dreams and visions. God came to Abraham after a "deep sleep" had fallen on him. Joseph was prominent both as a dreamer and an interpreter of dreams. Jacob had two life-changing dreams: the famous "ladder" dream and the one in which he wrestled all night with a supernormal being. In fact, it was because of this dream that his name was changed to Israel, symbolizing that he was a new person as a result of his encounter with God. Gideon got his military strategy in dreams. Saul, deprived of dreams, went to a witch for revelation. In a dream the Prophet Nathan was told that King David was not to build the Temple. It was in a dream that God asked Solomon, "What shall I give you?" and Solomon made his renowned request for "wisdom." In a dream Elijah was comforted by an angel after a run-in with Jezebel. And there are more dreams in the Book of Psalms, Job, Daniel, and so on.

In the New Testament dreams play an important role in the nativity story of Jesus: the Annunciation to Mary, and the assurance given to Joseph before Jesus' birth. And, after his nativity, Joseph is warned in a dream to escape to Egypt, later to return, and again to avoid Judea on their return.

Dreams and their meaning were important in the life of the early Christian Church. Morton Kelsey says that "every major Father in the early Church, from Justin Martyr to Irenaeus, from Clement and Tertullian to Origen and Cyprian, believed that dreams were a means of revelation."[1] In the fourth century, Kelsey tells us, "the great saint and mystic, Gregory of Nyssa, recognized that there was a close relationship between the art of Christian meditation and the experience of dreaming in sleep."[2]

Later, particularly in the Age of Reason, dreams were no longer so highly regarded. It remained for Dr. Sigmund Freud and his *The Interpretation of Dreams* to awaken the world once more to their power and significance. Later, Dr. Carl Jung helped us to understand that dreams also have spiritual implications and reveal powers of human perception. The purpose of dreams, according to Jung and others, is to make us whole.

---

[1]Kelsey, *Other Side of Silence,* p. 167.
[2]Kelsey, *Other Side of Silence,* p. 126.

As we indicated in chapter 7, we cannot really be whole if our conscious and unconscious minds are not on speaking terms.

Dr. David F. Dinges, Co-Director of the unit for experimental psychiatry at the Institute of Pennsylvania Hospital, believes that it's very likely that our bodies don't need sleep — our bodies need rest after labor, but they don't necessarily need sleep. Furthermore, he is convinced that the brain forces sleep on us because the brain needs sleep.

Since dreaming is a significant part of the sleep cycle, it would seem evident that dreams are not the "mental garbage" many have assumed them to be, but a therapeutic process which the mind demands. In laboratory tests it has been demonstrated that, when people are deprived of their dreams through EEG monitoring and awakened whenever it indicates the onset of a dream state, they soon become disoriented, confused and unable to function. They may even begin to experience emotional breakdown.

We believe that dreams are intended to make us whole, to prepare us for our daily rebirth, to restore the balance between the conscious and unconscious — in short, to help us get ourselves together. Very few, if any, of the dreams in the Bible are theological. Essentially, they are practical, their purpose being to help people meet the problems of daily living. Much of our experience with dreams has been precisely that kind.

Of course, there are different ways in which dreams can help us. Dreams may reveal consciously unrecognized truths about ourselves. Several decades ago, Valere had a recurring dream in which she saw herself putting the chopped-up body of a particular in-law down the garbage disposal in the sink. It was not a gory dream — no blood or obvious violence — but disturbing to her all the same. She was shocked when the dream first occurred and she continued to feel very guilty every time the dream returned.

Eventually, however, she began to realize that her dream was telling her something very important about some unconscious feelings she had not wanted to admit to herself. This particular in-law was daily putting a lot of pressure on Valere, constantly telling her what to do, how to run her life, how to raise her children, and so on. Valere had obviously assumed that one should not feel resentful of such a person and had therefore buried her hostilities so that even she, herself, was not aware of them. Finally, she recognized these buried feelings, so dramatically depicted in her dream, and began to accept them as not being "so terrible" under the circumstances. Brought to her consciousness, she was able to confront the problem and the dream stopped.

Another type of dream which is of practical help to us is the guidance dream. This kind of dream helps us toward making a decision or performing an action — something which presumably our unconscious mind already knows but the conscious mind doesn't. An example comes from the first year of our marriage. For some time, Larry had been deliberating over the question of whether or not to return to the pastorate. He did not want to leave the United Methodist ministry, but neither did he want to leave Dallas, where, because of an oversupply of ministers, there were no opportunities for him. How to stay in both Dallas and the ministry at the same time? That was the question.

For two nights in a row, just before going to sleep, Valere asked for the answer to this dilemma in a dream. The first night's "answer" was inconclusive, although encouraging. In this dream we were walking along a path when suddenly Larry spied a huge diamond lying on the ground, whereupon he picked it up and presented it to Valere. This "find" was very pleasing to both of them. But it was the second night's dream that ultimately proved so helpful. In this dream, Valere saw us at the groundbreaking ceremony. In the ceremony, the new foundation was to be poured. In the middle of the foundation was a strong metal center. We were very happy during this ceremony because we knew the building was to be ours.

Remembering that dreams frequently utilize a pun or play on words, when Valere related her dream to me, I recognized a possible play on the double meaning of the word "foundation." One of the ideas I had entertained, although not shared with Valere, was the formation of a religious *foundation* which could employ us both in our shared ministry of counseling, teaching, and writing. When I told her what I had been thinking, we both felt that, although she had dreamed of a material *foundation* for a building, the *foundation* was really to be the organizing principle for our ministry.

We did not know, however, what was meant by the "strong metal center" Valere had seen. Later in the week, I happened to mention what we were considering to a member of the staff of First United Methodist Church of Dallas, where we were currently attending and teaching a Sunday school class. One of the problems with which we were wrestling, as I said, was the question of how to link our foundation to the organized church in some way so Larry could continue to hold his credentials. It did not seem possible with a private *foundation*.

We seemed to have reached an impasse until Dr. Ben Oliphint (now Bishop), pastor of First Church, came to us, saying he had heard of our intentions to form a foundation, and was suggesting instead that we make our proposed New Dimensions Foundation a part of First Church and call it the New Dimensions *Center*. By *centering* it in the church, he said, the church would provide us with the strong undergirding that we would need. We accepted his proposal on the spot.

Another kind of dream is the warning dream. Sometimes these are precognitive, warning us about something of which we cannot be aware. Valere once dreamed that she was driving her car and Tammy, our daughter, was with her on the front seat; Neill, our son, asleep on the backseat. Suddenly a large truck smashed into the car and she knew that all three of them were killed. The dream was so frightening that she seriously considered cancelling her plans to drive to see her mother later in the week. Several days later, however, she set off as planned with Neill and Tammy accompanying her. The trip (approximately 100 miles) was uneventful.

On the way home however, she began to think about the dream again. Tammy was beside her on the front seat and Neill was asleep in the back. The "coincidence" of the scene in her dream led her to drive with increased vigilance. And it was this vigilance that probably saved their lives when a huge truck veered over the center line of the road and headed for them. Valere had just enough time — probably measured in the fraction of a second — to avoid a broadside and, although the truck did hit the car, the damage was nothing more than a crumpled fender — a miracle in view of the monstrous size of the truck and the speed at which it was travelling. You may call it a coincidence, if you like; Valere cannot.

But warning dreams do not have to be prophetic. They may simply tell you what you should be realizing and are not. One day following a lecture on dreams which she delivered to a woman's group in Dallas, Valere was called by one of the women who had been present. She wanted a private appointment with Valere to talk about her son's recurrent nightmares. During the session a few days later, the woman said that her son kept dreaming he was being hammered into the ground by little red devils with huge mallets. Almost every night since they had moved to Dallas he woke up screaming and crying.

"Tell me a little about him," Valere encouraged the mother. Until recently, when they moved from the country, the six-year-old boy's life had been very quiet and almost dull. In the country he had no playmates and spent most of his time alone. "But, since we've moved to the city," beamed the woman, "that's all been changed. Even though he never had been to kindergarten, we started him right off in first grade." She went on to tell proudly of how they had programmed the lad's time: Monday night, Indian Guides; Tuesday night, the church's Children's Choir, and so on: every day and night of the week was covered with some kind of organized activity. "You don't have any idea what his nightmare might mean?" asked Valere incredulously. "No I don't," was the woman's sincere reply. "Think for a moment," Valere said, "If someone were to take you out of a quiet, peaceful country setting into a big city and commit you to all kinds of programmed activities, wouldn't you feel as if you were being driven into the ground by something or someone?"

"That's absurd," retorted the mother, storming out the door, never to return (or pay). It appears that what she should have been able to figure out without the help of a dream, she repressed so hard that when the dream was explained to her, she still refused to receive the message.

There are also creative dreams. Valere once dreamed of toilet tissue on which were depicted images of dainty little flowers. If you don't think that's particularly creative, you need to consider it was just months before the first designer toilet tissue was marketed!

Many people have been blessed with creativity in their dreams. Mark Twain dreamed whole themes for his books. Robert Louis Stevenson got the idea for his *Dr. Jekyll And Mr. Hyde* in a dream, as did Mary Shelley her novel of *Frankenstein*. Among others who are reported to have gotten creative ideas in dreams are Benjamin Franklin, Voltaire, Thomas Edison, Mozart, John Newton, Albert Einstein, Edgar Allen Poe, and German scientist Frederick Kekule. Kekule's vivid dream gave him the clue to solving the problem that led him to invent the benzine molecule, leading him to exclaim, "Let us learn to dream, gentlemen."

Dreams may also be spiritual experiences. Twenty years ago, Larry was visiting in Nuremberg, Germany. The day had been frustrating and disappointing for him; it also seemed to stir up a lot of thoughts which he had left behind him in the USA. Although his outward circumstances were not bad, his inner feeling was one of despair and a sense of hopelessness.

He vividly remembers that he "awoke" in the middle of the night. The negative thoughts of the evening seemed to be waiting to pounce upon him and torment him anew. Suddenly, he was aware that someone was standing at the foot of his bed, just a bit to the left. Although he could not see much more than the outline in the darkness, he "knew" or "suspected" who it was. He felt afraid, but his fear was not a normal one. It was a "holy" fear. The figure, he was certain, was the Christ. He heard an authoritative voice say, "Be not afraid!" and with that the figure touched the bed, causing it to vibrate with a great intensity. After a while, the vibration stopped and the figure was gone, and with him Larry's fears and anxieties. This happened many years before Larry learned that the biblical term for "dreams" and "night visions" was often the same!

We have purposely shared dream examples from our own experience that appear to be simple and uncomplicated. Actually, the distinctions between kinds of dreams are not always so easily drawn. In fact, dreams can usually be interpreted on a number of different levels — all of them "right" and helpful.

Suppose you have a dream in which you see and/or feel yourself falling. On one level, you might approach this dream very literally. Is this a warning that you might actually have a physical mishap, a fall? On another level you might seek a play-on-words meaning. Perhaps the dream means that you are going to fall figuratively: a demotion in your job, an illness that may lay you low, a period of ill fortune (falling on hard times), and so forth. On still another level you might look for a symbolic message from your deepest realms: perhaps you're heading for a "fall from grace." On still another level, you might find the unconscious using the word or picture in an entirely unrelated manner: your dream may refer to the fall of the year, a person by the name of Fall.

If this is so, you may ask, then how can you know what the real meaning of the dream is? The answer is that some or all of these may be "real meanings" of the dream. Only you can determine what is "real" for you. Others can help you understand what your dreams may mean, but it's your dream and you must feel the "right" answer or answers.

Usually, when Valere speaks on this subject, we expect people to raise certain objections that seem to occur in every group. Assuming our readers are pretty much like our audiences, we will devote ourselves below to the most frequent questions directed to us.

- *I don't dream.* Someday we may discover that there are a few people who don't dream, but to date we have not. We believe everyone dreams, although lots of people do not remember dreaming. People who have claimed never to dream have been subjected to EEG brainwave monitoring and found to have REM (rapid-eye-movement) states just like the rest of us. The reason that the eye moves rapidly behind the darkness of the eyelid is that the unconscious mind is watching a dream scenario.

    Most people have from one to seven dreams per night or an average of 1,000 per year. A one-day-old infant has REM sleep 50% of the time, but as we grow older, the amount of time spent in REM sleep decreases somewhat.

    A night's sleep is normally a cycle of different levels of consciousness. When we first go to sleep, we usually go into a deep sleep. This first stage usually lasts about ninety minutes and is followed by a less deep level of REM sleep and a five-minute dream. Following this, we come nearly to the surface of consciousness before slipping into another period of deep sleep lasting approximately seventy-five minutes, followed by a dream of around fifteen mintues. As the night goes on, the length of the deep sleep shortens and the duration of the REM dreams lengthen. Thus, at our last dream, we are usually closer to consciousness and are more likely to remember it.

    Those who do not dream as much as others include people on sleeping pills, some mentally disturbed patients, people who have just eaten or drunk excessively, or those who are pretty much in touch with themselves with little or no pretensions and self-deceptions.

- *I can't remember my dreams.* That, of course, is what Valere told her course instructor. She and lots of others have learned, however, that we can train ourselves to remember our dreams. (See following section on techniques.) Frequently, when she has lectured on this subject, people have told her that they do not dream and, if they do, they don't remember. It never ceases to amaze us how many of these people come back or write to us the next day, confessing that the night after her lecture they not only dreamed but remember their dreams. One time, at a women's meeting, a woman became so hostile at Valere's statement that we all dream, that she nearly walked out of the meeting. The next morning, however, she was dumbfounded as she related that night's vivid and significant dream.

- *My dreams are just garbage.* We will certainly agree that lots of dreams seem that way: odd bits and pieces that appear to be meaningless and totally unconnected. Perhaps some dreams are composed of useless bits and pieces, but frequently we have found that the careful examination of the "garbage" can be very revealing. It may seem ridiculous for Larry to dream that he is back in school and finds, on the day of the big examination, that somehow he has failed to open the textbook throughout the course. Why should he remember and dream about something that is set so long ago? But, just as in those days the threat of not being prepared often hung over him, so there are times today when those old deeply-implanted memories are jogged by current situations in which he may not have "done his homework." The circumstances are different, but the old feelings are still there.

    Not only does the unconscious sometimes use old memories to lift up current problems, but it may also utilize unrelated data from our current experience to dramatize a concern that is totally unrelated to the items in the dream. The unconscious is like a playwright within us who creates problem-related dramas, using unrelated characters, situations, and locales the same way a bird uses miscellaneous bits and pieces to fashion a nest.

- *My dreams are too fragmented.* Although there are differing opinions on this subject, it seems to us that most often it is our remembrance, not our dream, that is fragmented. Just like recollections of events we experience with the conscious mind. Often, when we awake from a dream, we are aware that there was considerably more than we remember.

- *I can't understand my dreams.* But this does not mean that they have no meaning. It may mean that you simply haven't given enough time or thought to understanding them. It may also mean that you are resisting that understanding. The reason that some dreams are recurring dreams is that they have a message that is not being received. Some people don't want to understand themselves because they are afraid of what they will find. Others are introspective and have less difficulty in looking within and understanding what they find there. Haven't you ever tried to explain something to someone and been amazed that something so simple was still escaping their understanding? You can understand your dreams if you want to, and are willing to work at it.

- *My dreams disturb me.* Dreams are frequently disturbing. We know that. But we have also found that they are less likely to disturb us when we have worked with them and have better come to understand the nature and form of dreams. We have learned that there are some universal dream symbols that do not mean what they may seem to mean. If you dream that you kill someone, it does not mean that that is going to happen or that you are even considering it. It probably means you have very hostile feelings, but that is no reason to get upset and feel guilty. Or you may dream that you are out in public and suddenly realize that you are naked. Normally, this has nothing to do with sex or hidden tendencies toward exhibitionism, but means instead that you are afraid people can see you without your protective covering. You are caught with your resources down and are unprepared. Other universal symbolic dream images include:

Flying: this is a desire to escape or get "above it all."

Falling: this is an anxiety dream; you have overreached yourself—gone too close to the edge of something.

Crossing a bridge: you are facing an important decision that takes you from one situation to another.

Trapped in a tight place: an anxiety dream that means somehow you've been situationally boxed-in.

Being chased: another anxiety dream. Something is pursuing you—perhaps your own frightening impulses.

Vainly looking for a room or place: searching for yourself or your place in life.

Damage to your house or car: this is usually anxiety about yourself or your body.

Being devoured by a wild animal: something is "eating" you up or eating at you.

Losing your purse, wallet or teeth: you may be worried about losing you masculinity or femininity.

HOW CAN YOU REMEMBER AND USE YOUR DREAMS?

First it is important to accept the belief that you *can* remember your dreams. Then it is necessary to program your unconscious to help you remember your dream. Just before you are ready to put out the light and go to sleep, tell yourself three times, slowly, deliberately and forcefully, TONIGHT I WILL REMEMBER MY DREAMS.

When you wake after a dream, immediately start thinking backwards, reviewing as much of the visual images as possible. Do not start to analyze the meaning of the dream; first, get as many of the details as you can. Ask yourself about the pictures in your dream, and try to remember how you felt in the dream: calm, anxious, detached?

If you are unsuccessful for several nights, don't give up (remember Valere's experience at SMU). After several unsuccessful nights, instead of saying, TONIGHT I WILL REMEMBER MY DREAMS, you may try writing it on a piece of paper three times and put the paper under your pillow. Keep working at it until you *do* remember your dreams.

Probably the best way to understand and program your dreams is to keep a dream workbook. This will require a spiral notebook that opens flat so that you can write on both sides. Place this, along with a pencil or pen, on your night table or somewhere where you can easily reach it upon awakening. You might also want to keep a small flashlight or penlight so that you don't have to put on a bright light. This is particularly wise when you're sharing either the bed or the room.

Save the last 15 minutes before going to sleep for programming your dreams. One way to do this is to put the following information in your journal for the day: the date and very briefly what you did and felt during the day. Just the high and low spots — don't get strung-out.

Then mentally work on your dream request. In the beginning, it may simply be to remember your dreams. Soon, however, you may want to do some problem-solving or ask for guidance in a dream. So, decide what you want your dream(s) to tell you. Write down the problem or the situation. What is the cause of it? What are some possible solutions? Clarify your requests. Be specific, not vague. When you've worked on this for a few minutes, write a one-line statement of the request. Write it simply, distinctly and print boldly. Read it, preferably aloud.

Put out the light. Close your eyes and relax. Use some deep breathing relaxation, or some progressive relaxation if necessary. When you are relaxed and drowsy, fix your attention on the one-liner, repeating it over and over again in a passive manner as you fall asleep. Forget everything else you've written but the one-line statement of your request. Fall asleep with your request floating in your consciousness. If you dream and it's not a clear answer to your request, try again. It may take several dreams until you find your answer.

Sometimes sharing and discussing dreams can be an excellent means of communicating with others close to you. For example, you may be able to tell your spouse or child a dream (one whose meaning is clear to you), and by doing so, raise a subject that you might find otherwise difficult to discuss. When you discuss your dreams it is often easier to talk about your feelings. Encouraging your children to share and discuss their dreams is also an excellent way of keeping the lines of communication open. Instead of burying your head in the newspaper, at breakfast, why not ask someone, "What did you dream last night?" Young children particularly delight in telling their dreams. It is also a good way to get at some of their fears and anxieties.

*   *   *

One of the oldest written documents in the world (perhaps *the* oldest) is an Egyptian book of dream interpretations which has been dated at 3,000 B.C. and is now in the British Museum. It contains the following prayer:

> *God Mamu of my dreams. . .*
> *My God, send me a favorable message.*

RESOURCES FOR FURTHER STUDY AND SELF-DEVELOPMENT

Anon. *Dreams: A Key to Your Secret Self.* New York: Dell, 1963.
Bro, Harmon. *Dreams in the Life of Prayer.* New York: Harper & Row, 1970.

Farraday, Ann. *Dream Power.* New York: Berkeley Medallion, 1972.

———. *The Dream Game.* New York: Harper & Row, 1974.

Kelsey, Morton. *God, Dreams and Revelation.* Minneapolis: Augsburg, 1974 (originally published in 1968 as *Dreams: The Dark Speech of the Spirit*).

Loman, Eve. *You Are What You Dream.* Greenwich, CT: Fawcett, 1972.

Sanford, John. *Dreams: God's Forgotten Language.* Philadelphia and New York: Lippincott, 1968.

———. *Dreams and Healing.* New York: Paulist Press, 1978.

Sechrist, Elsie. *Dreams: Your Magic Mirror.* New York: Cowles, 1968.

IMAGERY:
SEEING AND DOING
WITH THE MIND'S EYE

Of all the things we do in our own lives as well as in our work with others — relaxation, meditation, stress management, dream work, healing and so forth — there is nothing we've used longer than imagery or visualization. That is, until the last few years. But we will come back to that shortly.

When she was five years old Valere came down with a very severe case of scarlet fever. The fever continued for days and gave no signs of breaking. Her hair, which she remembers distinctly as "thin and straight," fell out. She went into a coma and her physician called in two specialists. Although the physicians thought she was unconscious, Valere remembers very well their visit: "They had me in the dining room in a small bed, I guess to keep me isolated from the rest of the family. When I 'awoke,' I saw the two strange doctors, but not from my bed. Instead, I found myself looking down at them from a point at the ceiling in the corner of the room. And there, next to them, was my bed — and ME! I could see myself sleeping or unconscious. My mother and father were also in the room and I heard one of the doctors say, 'I'm sorry, there's just nothing we can do for her.' They didn't say I was going to die, but I knew that's what they meant. I can remember saying to myself something like, 'That's what you think! God, I guess it's up to us. I'm sure we can do it!' " Valere and God had that simple, informal kind of relationship that comes so easily to children and often seems so difficult for adults.

Valere remembers, "I didn't know the word imagery or visualization then, but I began to form a picture in my mind of me being well and with my hair back—but instead of thin and straight, I saw my hair as beautifully curly."

Soon after, Valere's fever broke and she began to get well. The doctors were doubly confounded, not only that she was going to live, but that she had survived without any brain damage resulting from the fever. Within a month, her hair began to grow back, but this time it was *beautifully curly*! And still is.

Valere shares another first-hand experience: "Tammy was seven when this happened. She, Neill and I were visiting a neighbor. The two of them were playing outside with the neighbor's children while I had a cup of coffee in the kitchen. The children's playful chatter suddenly turned to screams and Laurie, my neighbor, and I raced to the kitchen door. The children were screaming so that it was difficult at first to find out what had happened.

"Until we looked at Tammy. She was the only one not in hysterics. Instead, she seemed rather bewildered as she held her hand to her cheek. When she moved her fingers, I saw a hole where her cheek had been. Our neighbor's black Labrador had bitten her and taken away most of her cheek.

"Now Laurie was in hysterics, too. I grabbed her phone and called Tammy's pediatrician. 'Get the best plastic surgeon in Dallas and meet me right away at Baylor Hospital emergency.' When I hung up, Laurie was still hysterical and I had to slap her so she could help me put Tammy in the car.

"A few blocks away we encountered a policeman in a patrol car. 'Can you escort us to Baylor Hospital?' I asked, 'My daughter's been bitten by a dog.' In one of those now-just-calm-down voices, he said, 'You better let me see it.' He took one look at Tammy and exclaimed, 'O my God! Get in my car!' and we left my car standing in the middle of the street.

"When we arrived at the emergency room, the pediatrician and the plastic surgeon were waiting for us and it took 53 stitches and some intricate wiring to close the hole on the side of Tammy's face. 'You're very lucky,' the surgeon told me, 'one centimeter closer and your daughter would either be blind or that side of her face would be paralyzed. I've done the best I can, but she's going to have some indentation there for the rest of her life. There just wasn't enough cheek left.'

"I was grateful for his skill, but I silently disagreed with his prognosis. From the moment I first saw Tammy standing at the kitchen door, all the way to the hospital and while he worked on her, I kept visualizing Tammy grown up, in her graduation cap and gown, and just the thinnest hairline scar on the side of her face."

We've watched Tammy through two graduations with the satisfaction of knowing that only upon close examination can that thin hairline scar be seen on her right cheek.

We take nothing away from the plastic surgeon's skill, but neither do we doubt for a moment that Valere's mental picture of Tammy with the hairline scar contributed substantially to the fortunate outcome of the accident. Nor do we doubt that another mental image — Tammy as a high school cheerleader — also played a helpful, healing role some years later when she suffered a terrible spiral break in her leg as a result of a skiing accident. Once again the prognosis was dismal and the results were phenomenal. (Tammy *did* become a cheerleader, but gave up skiing.)

Larry also used imagery and visualization for many years, but often with a sense of intellectual discomfort. Although he regards himself as pretty much a pragmatist and works by the principle, "If it works, use it," he was sometimes nagged with the suspicion that visualization was nothing more than imagination (and, of course, we all know how disreputable that is!). Maybe the good results are simply coincidental. Even when he eventually rationalized how imagery might help the person doing it, how could it possibly be of any help to someone else?

All this visualization experience occurred before we had even a clue as to why or how imagery worked. It did seem to work — not always and not like magic — but haven't you ever had a headache that didn't respond to aspirin? We still can't prove that visualization works in all the ways in which we use it, but in recent years a fair amount of data on the successful use of imagery has been published. It is presently being employed as an adjunctive measure in medical therapy. A Dallas, Texas husband-and-wife team of psychologists, Dr. Jeanne Achterberg and Dr. G. Frank Lawlis, have published the results of extensive research which indicates that in a large number of diseases and injuries, people who display positive, hopeful imagery of their condition and their therapy get well faster and more surely. Not only that, but the doctors noted that the patient's imagery enabled them to predict both survival and non-survival. They also found that, often, when there was a change in imagery — from doubtful to hopeful — there was a greater likelihood of patient recovery. (More on this research in chapter 11.)

How does visualization or imagery work? Let's recall some of the points we've already explored in previous chapters:

- All or most thinking originates in the unconscious.

- All or most behavior is motivated in the unconscious.

- Dreams, visions, inner voices, and much creativity are lodged in the unconscious.

We also need to add the following:

• Images and symbols are the principal data of the unconscious mind and the conscious mind is highly responsive to these pictures as well.

We think in pictures for the most part, even when we're not aware of the images in the mind's eye. Proponents of Neuro-Linguistic Programming have made a study of people's bodily responses when they are in the midst of deep thought. Frequently, people unconsciously look away from the person with whom they are speaking, as if their eyes were looking at an invisible screen containing the answer to a question or the argument needed to continue the discussion. This, NLP people say, is because many people are actually imaging their ideas as pictures in the mind's eye.

Many of our words are, in effect, word-pictures — including some of what we regard as abstract ideas. These pictures exert tremendous influence over both mind and body. If you are shown a picture that is sexually stimulating, you most likely feel an effect upon your physical body. The picture in your mind's eye results in an electrical response in the nervous system, triggering a chemical reaction in the endocrinological complex, ultimately producing, in all probability, a response from one or more organs in the body.

People in advertising rely on this same kind of body/mind interrelationship when promoting the sales of food and drink. They are counting on the fact that their pictures "look good" to you — good enough to cause you to salivate and therefore motivate you to buy the product. Even advertising without pictures stimulates images.

We have long known about the mysterious efficacy of placebos. A placebo is a substance with no intrinsic therapeutic value that produces therapeutic results when patients believe the placebo to be a bonafide medication. The old "sugar pill" and its more sophisticated offspring have mystified a lot of doctors and healed a lot of patients — 30 percent says Dr. Herbert Benson.

But how does it work? Obviously it must be the belief of the patient, not the valueless pill, that triggers a beneficial response within the body. And what image alone can elicit this belief? Not the pill itself, but the *image* of a pill! The pill is so highly regarded and valued in our society that its image alone is able to set off in our bodies a host of neurological and endocrinological responses that have the capacity to heal. A negative example of the imagery power of mind over body is provided by Dr. Thomas Holmes of Washington University. In a project, sample biopsies were taken of subjects before and after discussion of certain subjects. Observes Dr. Holmes, "We caused tissue damage just by talking about a mother-in-law's coming to visit."[1]

We have illustrated the uses of visualization in taking charge of the body, but visualization is no less effective in helping you take charge of your psyche. You cannot change your behavior until you change the way you think—the way you perceive, how you feel about it, what it means to you. It is difficult for an overweight person to successfully manage a diet as long as he or she holds in the mind's eye a self-image that is "fat." No matter what he or she knows about the dangers of overweight with the conscious mind, that unconscious picture of a "fat" self will continue to direct the person's behavior.

So imagery can be a vital means of changing your perceptions and attitudes, and when you change these, you can also change your behavior. It is the failure to understand this that leads so many people to experience failure with willpower. Usually, willpower does not overcome unconscious conditioning until or unless it changes the inner picture or pictures that motivate you. Bad habits are broken, not so much by willpower, as by the substitution of a good habit in place of the bad. And good habits are formed mainly by motivational pictures in your mind's eye.

---

[1]From "Stress: Can We Cope?" *Time*, June 6, 1983. p. 49.

As we will explore further in chapter 12, imagery can also help improve relationships with other people because your visualizations can change your perceptions and attitudes about them. Changes in you often produce changes in others as well. Imagery also can be useful in improving your own self-esteem, the importance of which we discussed in chapter 2. It is your image of yourself that affects so much your own performance. If you have a "dunce" image implanted in your unconscious, you are not very likely to operate anywhere near your intellectual capacity!

When Larry was a sophomore in high school, he played football on the Junior Varsity team. Although he loved football, he didn't think he was much of an athlete and barely made the team — more by stubborn persistence than by demonstrated ability. Sometimes the Junior Varsity was ordered up to "the big field" to scrimmage with the varsity. "Cannon fodder" was the JV term for the experience.

On this particular afternoon, Larry was one of the JV linebackers on defense while the varsity showed off for the head coach. After fifteen or twenty minutes of rather unspectacular play, Larry happened to look over to the sidelines just in time to see his father arrive to watch the practice. Larry was dismayed; in his father's mind was the idea (a picture, actually) that Larry was a better player than he had been demonstrating up to that point. He would have to do something to keep that image intact.

On the very next play — a plunge through the center of the line — Larry managed to bring down the tough, big fullback after a mere one yard gain. The fullback looked surprised, but then so did Larry. On the next play — the quarterback must have decided the tackle was a fluke — the fullback again came roaring at the line. Having brought him down once, Larry didn't find it quite so difficult to bring him down again, this time at the line of scrimmage. Unfortunately, now both the fullback and the quarterback were annoyed. So the next play was a repeat performance, only this time Larry rushed across the line of scrimmage and brought the fullback crashing down for a two-yard loss.

There was a big pileup with Larry and the fullback on the bottom. Before lifting himself off Larry's chest, the fullback looked at him in disgust and said: "O.K. Althouse, why don't you tell your old man to go home so we can get back to normal!"

For an all too short period of time, his father's image of Larry's potential gave him the power to do what he had considered to be impossible. How often does self-doubt lock-up *your* storehouse of potential?

The use of imagery, therefore, can be a vital force in programming yourself to accomplish your goals. In sports today, for example, many athletes are learning to mentally rehearse their skills for the purpose of reaching maximum performance. If you sit perfectly still with your eyes closed and visualize yourself doing something physically active, the muscles that would have been used if the activity were real will respond somewhat, just as if the activity were actually happening. By "mentally rehearsing" many activities, you can better accomplish peak performance.

This is no less true in preparing yourself for other activities. For example, if you have to give a lecture, by mentally rehearsing it—seeing yourself doing it with ease, self-confidence, and good audience response—you are more likely to do your best in the actual performance. Or, let's suppose you are facing what you expect to be a difficult personal encounter. You may be afraid that you'll lose your temper, be intimidated, or forget what to say. Try mentally rehearsing the encounter and visualizing yourself doing exactly what you want to do.

Perhaps you have trouble saying "no" to people. You don't want to say "yes" and you don't intend to do so, but when you are face-to-face with that person, you just can't seem to do it. Later, you are angry with the other person as well as yourself. Probably you are unconsciously holding in your mind a picture that makes it difficult for you to say "no." So, mentally rehearse the encounter. Visualize yourself saying "no" firmly, but calmly. Visualize this over and over again, along with the feeling of how good it is to have maintained your resolution not to let this person take advantage of you.

Imagery can also be used to attract to you what you need. We realize this sounds somewhat "magical," but, although we cannot entirely explain how this might work, we are convinced that we have experienced it — and not by supernatural means. Actually, many people seem to attract to themselves what they really want out of life — fame, fortune, fun, favor, fatigue, and, although we're running out of "f's" the list could go on.

You know that wishing doesn't make it so. But when you so set your mind and heart — not to mention your unconscious resources — on the accomplishment of an objective that is within your capacities, often you are more likely to achieve that objective. What you have done is marshalled all your resources toward one goal, something you probably could not reach if you were less singleminded.

This singlemindedness — commonly held in the mind's eye as a visual goal — can also affect other people in the way they react to you. If you act as if you want something more than anything else in the world, they will often adopt your image of the goal and consciously or unconsciously co-operate. Of course, too much singlemindedness can also elicit hostility and opposition from others!

Today lots of people talk about "sending out" or "picking up" the "vibes" or "vibrations." For many it is just a figure of speech, but there are others who believe there is good evidence for believing that personality is manifested, not only in behavior, but also in emanations of energy that are not restricted to the physical limits of your own skin. (See this chapter's Resource list for reference to *The Body Electric*.) If there is any truth in this supposition — and we think it likely — you can also postulate that you are both a "sender" and a "receiver" of this energy, that energy may attract like-energy, and that some of what seems to "happen to you" may in some sense be what you have attracted to yourself.

Before we get into some techniques of imagery, let's first look at some guidelines:

1) Imagery works best when your body is relaxed and your mind passively alert. Therefore, imagery is often best used in conjunction with progressive relaxation and sometimes meditation.

2) You don't have to actually "see" the image in your mind's eye. Sometimes the conscious mind seems to resist certain images, but the unconscious mind does not heed its hangups. Just think about the image — that's enough — and whether or not you "see" it in your mind's eye is secondary. Of course, imagery is something that usually improves with practice.

3) That which is most familiar to you — especially people — is often the hardest to visualize pictorially. This is partly because the people who are closest to you are seen by you in a variety of moods, experiences and settings. It's easier to make a visual caricature of someone with whom you are less familiar. If you are experiencing temporary trouble in visualizing someone, focus on a feature of that person — eyeglasses, ski-jump nose, double chin, etc. If even that doesn't work, just use his or her name. It is easy to visualize words.

4) If you are going to visualize something or someone, whenever possible, study that thing or person so that the image may be imprinted on your mind. You won't remember what you see very well because you don't give the image any concentration. For example, at this moment Valere and I are looking at a photograph of Badgastein. If we glance at it, we come away with a vague image of an alpine town nestled among some mountains. But, if we want to use that picture for visualization, we must take some time to notice details — the red church steeple on the right, the mantle of snow on the mountain in the

foreground, the bright flowers on the Kongresscenter in the middle of the photo, and so forth. If we close our eyes and visualize the photo, we will not necessarily see all those features, but they will help us to form a stronger image in our mind.

5) Use as many of your five senses in the visualization as you can. Smell the flowers, feel the warmth of the sun, hear the birds, taste a blade of grass, as well as see the scene. The image will be strengthened in your mind's eye.

6) Always use positive images and affirmations. For example, if you are using imagery to help control your appetite, it is much better to visualize yourself feeling satisfied and nourished, than picturing yourself throwing up because of what you've eaten! The negative image may accomplish the task, but it may also leave some unfortunate associations that cause you trouble later.

7) When doing affirmations — a kind of visualization that stirs images with words — address yourself by name.

8) Don't let dark or contradictory thoughts upset you. As in meditation, your response is passive. You do not resist or fight them — which would give them more strength — but you simply let them float by.

9) Choose your pictures carefully. Don't visualize something you really don't want. In today's *International Herald Tribune* there's a "Peanuts" cartoon that illustrates this beautifully. In the first frame we see little Lucy praying by her bed. In the second frame she is walking away. In the next two frames she explains to Linus why she broke off her prayers: "I was praying for greater patience and understanding, but I quit. . . . I was afraid I might get it."

10) Don't play God. Imagery should not be used to manipulate other people, to "magically" control events, or to impose your own ideas on your world. Shakti Gawain tells readers that it is

not necessary to believe in metaphysics or spiritual ideas in order to use imagery. That is true, you *can* do it without scruples, but you *ought not* to leave God or some standard of ethics out of the picture. The near tragedy of "The Sorcerer's Apprentice" is the fate of many who try to play God.[2]

HOW CAN WE LEARN TO VISUALIZE AND USE IMAGERY?

You can prove to yourself that you can visualize by performing any or all of the following exercises. Remember first to relax your body and let your mind become passively alert.

1) Close your eyes and see in your mind's eye a tv or motion picture screen. It is first blank. Then, watch it turn totally red. Observe the redness and then watch it turn orange. Then yellow, blue, green, purple, brown, black and gold. Now open your eyes.

2) Close your eyes and visualize your bedroom. Stand in the doorway and look around the room from one direction to the other. Notice items of furniture. Look at some of the personal items on the furniture: your watch, eyeglasses, articles of clothing, and so forth. Examine the floor and then the ceiling. Look at the light fixtures, the windows, blinds, drapes. Walk over to

---

[2]The "Sorcerer's Apprentice" is a folk tale that was set to music by Dukas and later became a sequence in Walt Disney's motion picture, *Fantasia*. It is the story of a sorcerer's apprentice who, eager to graduate from menial tasks in the laboratory and get on with performing magic, tries out some of the master's formulas while the sorcerer is away and succeeds in getting furnishings and tools to dance around the room. But, as the pace gets faster and faster, the apprentice finds he doesn't know how to stop it and only the timely arrival of the sorcerer averts complete tragedy.

your bed and lie down on it. Feel the give or hardness of the mattress. Look around the room from your bed. Then open your eyes.

3) Decide on a peaceful scene — the seashore, the mountains, your garden, whatever. Now close your eyes and see that scene, first in total, then in detail. Use all five senses to experience the scene. Note the feeling of peace and serenity you feel here. Know that you can return here for renewal any time you want. Then open your eyes.

4) Visualize a recent pleasant experience — eating your favorite food, swimming, skiing, making love, resting in a hammock, and so forth. See the scene and then feel once again the sensations of pleasure. What was the texture of the food? How did the water feel? And, well, you get the idea. Then, open your eyes.

To work out your visualization program, first set your goal. Start with an easy goal the first few times. Be realistic. Then decide on the image, or images, you will use. You may be able to use a photograph (yourself, for example, when you were leaner and more fit), or you may have to create your picture mentally. Take time to decide what will be in it. Determine a schedule for using it. Three times per day is a minimum and, like meditation, it works best if you set aside the same time every day or in conjunction with the same activity. In addition to this, remind yourself to use it on a random basis whenever you have a moment — waiting in the doctor's office, eating lunch alone, and so forth. Keep the pictures as personal and simple as possible. Don't use abstractions. See yourself acting in a loving way to someone rather than "feeling loving to whom it may concern."

It's important to decide on the length of the project period. How long will you continue to practice this visualization before you evaluate your results or examine your program for possible changes? Make sure you give it enough time — Rome wasn't visualized in a day! Make sure you have suspended your doubts, that you have the desire to reach your goal, but be flexible enough to accept results that may not come in just the form you intended. In other words, don't be like the woman who prayed for patience and then complained bitterly because God sent her a sloppy maid.

Sample Exercises

Visualization for improving self-esteem: In your mind's eye, visualize someone you respect or whose approval and opinion you value. Hear them tell you some of the things they like about you.

Or: visualize yourself before a large audience. See and hear them giving you a rousing round of applause. See yourself bowing and acknowledging their acclaim. (If you really need a shot in the ego, see them standing on their feet and shouting "Bravo! Bravo!")

Visualization for improving memory: In your mind's eye see yourself sitting in front of a home computer. It is composed of two units: a typewriter-like keyboard and a tv-style screen. The computer represents your personal memory bank. It holds all the things your mind has recorded. Find the on/off switch and turn it on. Ask yourself a simple question, like "Who is my next door neighbor?"

Watch yourself type that question and see it appear on the screen. When you have typed the question and the question mark, look to the right of the keyboard and find a large key marked "Recall." Press this key and hear the computer click, hum, murmur for a few moments, until it has found your answer in the memory bank. Hear the computer give a "beep" sound as you watch it write the answer — your neighbor's name — on the screen. Watch yourself do this five times, each time using an easy question, and feeling the satisfaction as the answer appears on the screen.

By doing this visualization you are persuading yourself that you have a good memory that can recall whatever is stored in it. When you complete the visualization, give your computer a gentle pat, and say, "I've got an excellent memory," three times. Lots of people unwittingly program a poor memory by telling themselves and others, "I've got a lousy memory — always have and it's getting worse all the time."

If you want to do more work in this area, see chapter 11 for some healing visualizations, or chapter 12 for visualizations you can use in interpersonal relationships.

RESOURCES FOR FURTHER STUDY AND SELF-DEVELOPMENT

Achterberg, Jeanne & Lawlis, H. Frank. *Bridges of the BodyMind.* Champaign, IL: Institute for Personality and Ability Testing, 1980, (*The* book on imagery.)

_____. *Imagery in Healing.* Boston: New Science Library, 1985.

_____. *Imagery of Cancer.* Champaign, IL: Institute for Personality and Ability Testing, 1978.

Gawain, Shakti. *Creative Imagery.* New York: Bantam, 1979.

Green, Elmer and Alyce. *Beyond Biofeedback.* New York: Dell, 1977.

Moss, Dr. Thelma. *The Body Electric.* Los Angeles: J.P. Tarcher, 1980.

Pelletier, Kenneth R. *Mind As Healer — Mind As Slayer.* New York: Dell, 1977, Chapter 7.

Rossman, Martin, M.D. *Healing Yourself.* New York: Walker, 1987.

Samuels, Mike, M.D. and Samuels, Nancy. *Seeing With The Mind's Eye.* New York: Random House, 1975.

CHAPTER

10

INTUITION
AND OTHER POWERS
OF THE MIND

Valere has always been intuitive — just as we all are. The difference is that she has known, accepted and used these powers since as early as she can remember. As a little girl in Buffalo Springs, Texas, she frequently knew of things that were happening or going to happen because the thoughts, often in the form of pictures, came into her mind. At first, she assumed that everyone had and used this channel of knowing. Valere tells of one of her earliest remembered experiences: She was seven or eight when this happened. At that time her paternal grandmother lived with the family. She remembers walking in the house one day and blithely announcing to her grandmother, "Maggie Lee is going to New York to see her father."

"How do you know she's going to New York?" she wanted to know. "Did she tell you?"

"No," Valere replied innocently, "I'm not even sure she knows yet. I guess I just saw it in my head."

Her grandmother didn't comment for a little while. Then she said: "I don't think you should tell just anybody about this — seeing things in your head, that is."

Valere was surprised. "Doesn't everyone see those things?" she asked.

"No," replied the grandmother. "It's a special gift from God."

There was another period of silence while Valere pondered that. Then her grandmother said, "What will you do if you see one of your little friends in an accident or even dying?" Her question frightened Valere. That evening after supper she remembers going out in the yard and sitting in the swing. It was a beautiful starry Texas night. She looked up at the stars and said, "God, I won't ever use this gift wrong, if you promise not to let me see death."

"I think we've both kept the bargain."

Valere sees many things intuitively, but never death. Several years ago a U.S. Senator and his wife had an appointment with her and she gave them several intuitive predictions, but no accidents, no imminent death. The next day they were both killed in a plane crash. On the positive side she has intuitions of undiscovered or unused personal potential, assistance with business decisions (never our own), assistance with personal problems, recovery of lost objects, and warnings about possible harmful conditions.

An example of the latter occurred during dinner at a friend's house some years ago. Our hostess told Valere that her husband, an engineer, had been invited to the White House as a consultant on some presidential project. Valere almost never shares an intuition unless she's asked, but when she looked at him, she blurted out: "Are you going to have a physical check-up before you go to Washington?"

"Are you kidding," replied her host, "I'm going to Washington tomorrow." Valere felt impelled to persist: "I don't know why, but I'm picking up that you may have some problem with your heart and you ought to get it checked out."

"There won't be time for that," he replied.

"Well," said Valere with unaccustomed doggedness, "try to get a check-up right after you get there." With that the matter was dropped for the rest of the evening. Approximately one month later, Valere got a letter from his wife. She was sorry for the delay in contacting Valere, but things had been hectic: on their third day in Washington her husband had had a heart attack. "He's going to be o.k.," she finished.

We have found that people are usually more receptive to good news than bad news. About fifteen years ago, Valere told one woman that she "picked up" that she was quite artistic and could do very well as an artist. The woman admitted that she used to paint, but hadn't for years. In view of serious arthritis and other complications, it was not very likely she'd ever use another paintbrush. But, within approximately one year, she started painting again and found her paintings very much in demand. She was given many commissions and eventually held several very successful exhibitions.

Later, she returned to ask Valere's advice concerning a pending marriage. Although Valere had never met the man, she told the woman that she had grave doubts about the prospective groom. "I can't help telling you I feel he's after your money and will only make you very unhappy." Nevertheless, the woman went through with the marriage, which lasted less than two months. It was enough time, however, for the groom to take his bride "to the cleaners."

Valere seems to have an intuitive affinity for other people's artistic potential. At the Greenhouse, a spa in Arlington, Texas where for fourteen years she did weekly lectures and counseling, Valere met a wealthy socialite who was just plain bored with life. "You are really very artistic," said Valere, "something you do with your hands." The woman was dubious, but admitted when in college she had done a little sculpting. "Well," Valere responded, "I think you could do a lot with it." About two years later, Valere received an announcement of a private showing of the woman's sculptures. At the bottom the woman had written: "Thanks to you, Valere."

On one occasion, Valere's detection of artistic potential was unknowingly *after* rather than *before* the fact. One of her Greenhouse appointments was a striking woman from California. She was a new client and her name was not familiar to Valere. Valere told her a number of things about her life and family and, as the interview neared its conclusion, Valere added, "Oh yes, I also believe you are quite talented and could pursue a career singing or acting, but it's your voice I keep picking up." Noncommitally the woman smiled and said, "I'll think about that." Later that week, Valere discovered that her client's professional name (not used during the session) was that of one of the nation's top female recording stars!

Valere told another woman that she saw big changes in life — geographically, professionally and personally. "I see you travelling a lot and working with famous people, mostly outside the USA."

"Well," said the woman, "my husband's about to retire, so that might explain the travel part, but I can't place the rest of it." A year or so later, the retired husband got a new camera as a gift and not much later both husband and wife found themselves totally engrossed in a second career as world-renowned society photographers. Valere received several notices of their exhibitions abroad and treasures a copy of a volume of their published portraits.

Intuitive capacities not only can give you valuable information from unknown sources, but intuition also serves as a medium of communication that lies beyond the powers of reason and the five known physical senses. In 1954, Valere was working for the American Medical Association in St. Louis, Missouri, in an outpatient program for treating emotionally disturbed people with either electric-shock or insulin therapy. Because the psychiatrists did not have sufficient time to work with the patients, Valere's role was to serve as a liaison with the patients, gaining their confidence and engaging them in conversation that eventually might provide some helpful data for the doctors.

One of the patients with whom she had been unsuccessful was a physician who suffered a nervous breakdown several years previously and hadn't spoken a word since. One day, sitting with him and failing to elicit any response, without warning to either herself or him, she said, "Doctor, why do you blame yourself for that woman dying on the operating table?" There was a moment of terrible silence before he turned to her and said, "How the hell did you know that?" An intuition succeeded in opening the door to healing where electric-shock, insulin, and psychiatry had failed.

Sometimes intuition is just as helpful with less dramatic and vital matters. Several years ago while we were on a cruise of the Greek Isles, Larry's watch slid down behind a wooden partition in our cabin. We tried fishing it out with a bent coat hanger. We got an amazing assortment of items out of that crack, but not his watch. So, we called the steward and asked him to perhaps remove a panel to reach it. Dubiously he looked down the crack and said he would return later.

Several days went by, the steward had not returned, and Larry determined he would buy a small handsaw at Rhodes, the next port of call. He was determined to reclaim his watch. Valere looked dubious when he told her his plan, but said nothing. Later that afternoon they were on a bus bouncing its way between Lindos and Rhodes, Valere's head nodded forward in a momentary reverie. Then, opening her eyes and straightening up, she said, "Don't bother to get the saw. The steward's retrieved your watch and will be there to hand it to us when we get back." Inasmuch as he had previously witnessed the remarkable accuracy of these little reveries of Valere's, Larry decided to hold off on his purchase.

When they returned to the ship, he rushed to the cabin. Upon entering, however, there was no one there. Just as he was about to utter a significant "Aha!" there was a knock at the door. When he opened the door, there was the steward, holding his watch!

Just as Valere would confound her playmates by saying, "Evelyn, you brother's in a fight and he's going to come home all beat-up," so, she both intrigued and annoyed her own children with her occasional intuitive peeks into childhood deceptions. Once, while shopping with a friend, she turned and said, "I've got to go home right away; Neill needs me." Neill was twelve at the time. Upon arriving at the house, she found the family car gone. She paced up and down the sidewalk a few times until she saw the car turn the corner with Neill more or less in command of the wheel. After a less than practiced halt in the driveway against the neighbor's chimney, Neill slid out from behind the wheel and sulked into the house. "I should have known it! I should have known it! That's what I get for having a witch for a mother!"

Valere is not a witch, although from time to time bigoted and self-righteous "Christians" have said as much, forgetting, apparently, the tremendous store of intuitive and psychic experiences recorded in the Bible and the fact that in the early church this gift was recognized as prophecy.

Like most people, Larry used to say, "I'm not intuitive at all." But he has discovered that everyone has this God-given endowment to some degree. Sigmund Freud believed that ESP in human consciousness is the residue of an ancient mode of communication before humans developed the powers of speech. Recent left brain/right brain research indicates that intuitive thought is a function of the right side of the brain. In order to be balanced human beings, we need to use both rational and intuitive faculties. We hope to help you discover the intuitive and other powers of the mind that can be beneficial to you in living a richer, fuller life.

Larry has learned to use his intuitive powers. Several years ago he was trying to reach an author who was to lecture to a group with whom Larry was associated. When he called, Larry was informed that the phone number was no longer in service. Then Larry called an organization that he hoped would know the author's number. He learned the author moved to Cape Cod, but was given no city.

Calling the area information number for Cape Cod, Larry attempted to get the number, but the operator said she couldn't find it unless he knew the name of the city or town. "There are scores of communities on Cape Cod," she told him. Larry got out a road map of Massachusetts and looked up Cape Cod. "Let's see whether ESP will help me find it," he muttered and let his finger fall at random on a community on the Cape. Reading the name under his finger, Larry called the information operator, told her the name of the town and the author's name. "Just a minute," said the operator, "the number is. . .!" Within a few minutes Larry had his author on the line.

Sometimes your intuitive powers can help you find something more valuable than a phone number. A few years ago, Valere got a call from a friend who was calling because the wife of a wealthy industrialist had lost a very large diamond ring. The friend asked if Valere could help her find it. "You know I don't like to get involved in that kind of thing," Valere told her friend. "I'm not good at it, it's a hassle and often a thankless job."

"No," said her friend, "there's a sizable reward for finding it." Valere still refused, but finally, out of friendship, said, "I'll tell you what we'll do. Larry and I are going into meditation in a few moments and we'll see if we get any impressions. But that's all!"

Neither Larry nor Valere were very encouraged with what they got in meditation. Valere saw the ring in a long rectangular box and had the impression it was where it was supposed to be. "What did you get?" she asked Larry. "I hate to tell you," he replied, "all I saw was a large Boeing 747 taking off at an airport."

At the appointed time, the industrialist's wife called, "I will be very grateful if you can help me," she told us. Valere then proceeded to tell her what we had picked up. Her mood changed abruptly: "That's ridiculous! It can't be where it's supposed to be. This is a waste of time!"

That was the last we ever heard from her. A month or so later, Valere encountered someone who knew both Valere's friend and the woman who lost her diamond. "Valere!" she bubbled, "I heard about your remarkable hit in finding the missing diamond and that you got a big reward!"

"No," said Valere, "we have heard nothing." Disbelieving, the woman told us that the woman was giving her deposition to the police when her daughter walked in the house and wanted to know what was going on. When the mother told her about the loss of the diamond, the daughter said, "Mother, don't you remember? You gave it to me for safekeeping before you boarded the plane for Europe. It's in my safe deposit box, *where it's supposed to be.*"

Whenever we lecture on this subject, people usually have several reactions. On the one hand, we talk with many people who share their own intuitive experiences with us. Other people sometimes dismiss intuitive experiences as sheer coincidence. (Ironically, a few people have told us that they neither believe our experiences or the ones they have had either!)

For the past century, parapsychologists have compiled an impressive mass of data demonstrating that some people have what appears to be an extrasensory means of communicating with others, obtaining information through unknown channels, and even exerting some influence of mind over matter. Dr. J.B. Rhine of Duke University and later the Foundation for Research on the Nature of Man, spent decades compiling massive evidence for precognitive ESP—foretelling something before it happens—and other types of psychic phenomena. Valere was one of Dr. Rhine's many tested subjects.

Recently some resource data has been published that is significant for several reasons. The researcher is not a parapsychologist or psychical researcher. He is Dr. Robert G. Jahn, Dean of the School of Engineering and Applied Science at Princeton University. Dr. Jahn does not use the terms, parapsychology, psychic, or even ESP in his research at Princeton. Instead he calls it "Engineering Anomalies Research," a reference to research findings that do not fit into known scientific expectations. Dr. Jahn, his associate Brenda Dunne, and their staff have carried on research into two different areas. The first of these involves what Jahn and Dunne term "low-level psychokinesis — the interaction of human consciousness with some physical device, system, or process producing a behavior different from that expected on the basis of known science." Using a sophisticated machine called the "Random Event Generator," the experimentors have instructed a number of human operators to try to distort the distributions of the REG machines using the power of the mind to do so. Psychokinesis is popularly known as PK and represents the old concept of mind over matter. Sifting through data representing many tens of thousands of trials, the evidence clearly indicates that the operators were mentally able to affect the operation of the machines.

The second set of experiments is even more exciting, involving precognitive remote perception, or the acquisition of information from remote locations, inaccessible to any known sensory channels. In these experiments subjects, called "percipients," are asked to visualize or otherwise sense the details of a geographical target at a location that is physically remote. The specific picture which the percipient tries to sense is one chosen by another participant called the "agent." The percipient and agent have no contact with each other. Dr. Jahn's staff has worked out an elaborate schedule of criteria by which the accuracy of the percipient's answers can be rated. After analyzing the data of many, many trials, Dr. Jahn and his associates concluded that there was strong evidence for this remarkable power of the mind. But the most remarkable aspect of this study is that, in most trials, the percipient made his or her "hits" and "misses" at a considerable time *before* the agent selected the targets. Thus, we have evidence, not only for mind-to-mind communication, but also precognition.

Even more significant, perhaps, is the fact that in his Engineering Anomalies Research, Dr. Jahn and his staff have used only student volunteers who have no experience in ESP and are not recognized as specially-gifted. What this suggests is what we have been saying throughout this chapter: intuition and other powers of the mind are not the possession of a gifted few, but the common endowment of all of us. To be sure, there are those who are specially gifted and many more who have discovered and highly developed those potentials, but each of us can draw on this God-given faculty.

HOW CAN WE DISCOVER AND DEVELOP OUR POWERS OF MIND?

It is absolutely essential you believe that you have intuitive powers and can use them. If you believe that ESP works, you are more likely to be successful with it than if you do not. If you are a habitual (notice we did not say "born") skeptic, then at least approach the subject with the most productive of all scientific attitudes: *Let's give it a try and see what happens!*

Relaxation and meditation are the best preparation for the use of your intuitive powers. Seek the relaxed body and the passively alert mind. Don't approach the testing procedures we will discuss with a "do-or-die" attitude. If you are too aggressive or too intense about what you want to happen, you create a barrier to what is called the "psi flow."

Intuitive powers must be both accepted and exercised. A common reaction when you begin to receive something by intuition is to dismiss what you are getting as "just imagination." That will usually stop the flow. As your impressions begin to present themselves, receive them passively. Don't try to analyze them. There is plenty of opportunity for that later.

Get into the habit of trying out your intuitive sense in everyday experiences. When the phone rings, before you pick it up, decide who it will be. When you get a letter, before you look at the return address or open it, let your intuition suggest who your correspondent may be. If you are going to a party or a meeting, let your intuition suggest what your hostess will be wearing or the color(s) of her apparel; the same can be done with the chairperson of your meeting. Another type of individual practice is to send psi "messages" to people, asking them to write, call, or visit you.

Don't be discouraged if you don't get good results right away. For most of your life you have probably been educated and trained to distrust your intuition and to rationalize everything you do. It may take a while before you begin to get in touch with this faculty that for so long has had to hide in your unconscious. Children often do much better with intuitive powers because they don't know yet that they can't do these things.

Work with a psi-partner. Choose someone as a partner who is interested in working with intuitive power for a series of projects. The first of these is similar to the mind-to-mind communication testing done by Dr. Robert Jahn, although without the scientific controls used in the laboratory. Each week, or even several times a week, schedule a percipient (receiver) and agent (sender) exchange. The sender will take a certain period of time (five to ten mintues) to send to the receiver a word, symbol, or picture. These "targets" should not be items that you might expect each other to send. In scoring hits, misses, and scores in between, note that, as in your dreams, there may be a play on words or sounds. Targets that have an emotional intensity — anger, love, sorrow, etc. — are often easier to hit. Be alert for what is called "psi missing." Some people, instead of picking up the target you are sending them, regularly pick up the last one you sent or the next one you are about to send. This is evidence for psi, too, but we don't know why it happens.

A second psi-partner project may be done with what is called psychometry, the attempt to obtain information from the vibrations that emanate from objects. The psychometrist will hold an object in his or her hand and allow himself to receive impressions from the object's vibrations—information about who owned it, who gave it, and so forth. With a psi-partner it is well for the one partner to wrap the object (again, not one that might be expected) in tissue paper and place it in a box. We recommend using the same size box so the psychometrist cannot get a clue to the size of the object from the box. Have the psychometrist hold the box in his or her hands and verbalize whatever impressions he or she gets. When psychometrizing, give it plenty of time so the psi flow can start.

Our son, Neill, was a whiz at this at the age of seven. Once Valere put a little red racing car in the box, and Neill's impressions were of "streaks of red going very fast . . . there is a stripe of white in the red . . . " The racing car had a white stripe. On another occasion when the target was a Spanish piece-of-eight, Neill described accurately the irregular shape of this antique coin.

Some psi work can be done with small groups. For example, whenever she was to lecture on the power of intuition, Valere would call a neighbor and ask her to place an object on her mantle without telling what it was. Then, she would ask the group to try to pick up what the object was. When all the group's impressions were recorded, Valere would either call the neighbor or open a sealed envelope in which the name of the article was written.

Another project which may be used by groups involves PK—psychokinesis—mind over matter. When Tammy was a preschooler, Valere conducted several projects with Tammy and her classmates. She obtained some relatively fast-growing seeds, and put them in three boxes of earth. The boxes were exactly alike and each box received the same amount of seeds. All three boxes were placed in the same location in the dining room. Each day the three boxes received the same measured quantities of water and were exposed to the same quantities of sunshine. Tammy's class was divided into two groups. Group A was in charge of the first box; Group B the second; and the third box was the control—no one worked with it. Five days per week the preschoolers would come by the house. Each group was allowed two five-minute periods to love and talk to the seeds.

The project generated a lot of interest and excitement. Each day as they arrived, the children tried to determine which box of seeds was growing faster and bigger. If it seemed that Group A's seeds were ahead, that was usually a signal for Group B to exert more effort. Everyone could see, however, that box number three had the poorest response of all. At the end of ten days the sprouts were examined to see which had grown tallest and which had produced the most shoots. Because of the keen competition, the growth results were usually pretty close, but the seeds in box three produced shoots that averaged from one quarter to one third the size of shoots in boxes one and two.

"Scanning" may be done in groups where the people are not well-acquainted with each other. If they know each other, of course, they will be too influenced by what they already know. In scanning, there is a receiver, but no sender. The receiver stands in front of a person who does not attempt to "send" anything, but simply remains relaxed and passive in their attention. The receiver or scanner looks into the eyes of the subject, not for the purpose of seeing, but to focus on the personality of the subject. As impressions come to the scanner, he or she speaks them aloud. The subject should wait a few minutes before confirming or denying the impressions received by the scanner.

Larry did this one time at a meeting and became absolutely flabbergasted at the accuracy of the information he was getting. When he got too impressed with his information the flow stopped almost immediately!

A psi experience that can be used to get information from a remote location is sometimes called an OBE (out-of-body-experience) or travelling clairvoyance. The suggestion with both terms is that in some way the mind leaves the body and "sees" or otherwise experiences things at another physical locatiohn. One of our friends, Carol Ann Liaros, teaches blind people to "see" this way. That is, she teaches them to use their intuitive powers to "see" with the mind's eye what their physical eyes cannot see. Training in this technique, called the Blind Awareness Project, includes encouraging subjects to "travel" with their minds to a particular location and then to describe it. You, too, can use this method. If you are going to visit a place you've never been before, "travel" there mentally and view the location, writing down your specific impressions. Then, when you actually visit that location, check out your accuracy. Some people learn to do this very, very well. More information on Carol Ann Liaros and Blind Awareness is listed in the Resource section.

RESOURCES FOR FURTHER STUDY AND SELF-DEVELOPMENT

Ebon, Martin. *Test Your ESP.* New York: World Publishing, 1970.

————. *The Psychic Reader.* New York: World Publishing, 1969.

Heron, Laurence Turnstall. *ESP in the Bible.* New York: Doubleday, 1974.

Higgins, Paul Lambourne, ed. *Frontiers of the Spirit.* New York: T.S. Denison, 1976.

Johnson, R.C. *Psychical Research.* New York: Funk & Wagnalls, 1968.

Kelsey, Morton T. *The Christian & the Supernatural.* Minneapolis: Augsburg, 1976 (Good book, poor title.)

Leshan, Lawrence. *The Medium, the Mystic, and the Physicist.* New York: Viking Press, 1975.

Liaros, Carol Ann. *Practical ESP.* Buffalo, NY: PSI Search, 1985.

Moss, Dr. Thelma. *The Probability of the Impossible.* Los Angeles: J.P. Tarcher, 1974.

Sherman, Harold. *How To Make ESP Work For You.* Los Angeles: DeVorss, 1964.

————. *Your Mysterious Powers of ESP.* New York: World Publishing, 1969.

11

PATIENT, HEAL THYSELF!

Virginia — that's what we'll call her — was desperate. Her voice, if not her fortune, was at least her livelihood. All singers from time to time experience hoarseness, strain, and other impediments to getting the most out of their voices. It is as if their Achilles' heel is in their throats. But Virginia had been bothered by excessive hoarseness for the past nine months. The longer she remained hoarse, the harder it was to sing at her usual level; the harder it was to sing, the more anxious she became; and the more anxious she was, the more her voice continued to be hoarse and painful. She had been to several physicians, but her condition had not improved. Like so many people who come to us, she came because she was desperate and had nowhere else to go.

"I'll do anything if you can heal me," she said to Larry. "I may take you up on that," smiled Larry, "but I'm not going to heal you of anything." Knowing she was a deeply spiritual woman, he added: "God has already placed within you the power to heal yourself." There may have been a time when she might have argued that point with him, but now she was ready to do whatever he suggested.

He suggested that she begin a daily routine of relaxation, visualization, and meditation. She may have been a bit disappointed, thinking he was going to do something or give her something, but she was motivated to follow his instructions. Within a week or ten days, she called back to say her voice was fine. Perhaps a year later we heard from her again and she had never experienced any more difficulty with her throat or voice.

Another woman — we'll call her Donna — came to us with three problems. Her physicians had been unable to help her; she was diagnosed as having multiple sclerosis, a degenerative, crippling disease; she was subject to deep depressions (many mornings, she said, she was afraid to get out of bed); and she couldn't get pregnant. As she was currently a client at the Greenhouse, we met her several times for healing sessions. Mostly we taught her relaxation, meditation, and imagery, and we worked on the self-image that she was "hopelessly ill."

Within a month or so we got an excited phone call from her. The MS symptoms were gone — amazing her doctors — and she was winning her battle with depression. Now, if we could just work on her getting pregnant, everything would be wonderful. We assured her we'd continue sending her some "good thoughts." A few more months went by and we got another call from her, this time obviously ecstatic: she was pregnant! And she was giving all the credit to us!

It was not humility that made us decline the credit — or responsibility. Whatever she had accomplished with her supposed degenerative disease, her depression and infertility, she had done herself. We were not even really her "healers," for what we did was to help her remove the obstacles that kept her from utilizing her own healing powers within.

In saying, "Patient, heal thyself," we are not suggesting that self-healing be regarded as an alternative to medical treatment or diagnosis. We do encourage clients to seek a second opinion or question physicians on the what and why of a particular therapy. Some physicians look upon our work with their patients as a complementary therapeutic approach, and some have sent their patients to us from time to time. Some health professionals, such as the doctors and nurses we meet at the annual conference of the Holistic Nurses Association in Springfield, Missouri, have been very helpful in substantiating our own convictions about the body/mind/soul connection.

Whether by licensed physician, clinical psychologist, surgeon, nutritionist, spiritual healer or witch doctor — all healing is really self-healing. While not for a moment suggesting that the above are equal in their efficacy with the patient, each method can assist a patient to heal him- or herself using the marvelous self-healing systems and resources within. Sometimes there has to be an intervention — pills, radiation, scalpel, psychotherapy, laying-on-of-hands and so forth — but the intervention, whatever it is, does not heal. It merely allows the body to heal itself. It was a renowned physician, Dr. Alexis Carrel, who said, "I set the bone, but God does the healing." Whatever God you acknowledge — the Judeo-Christian Creator/Father, the Hindu pantheon or a cosmic Wholly Other — He/She/It heals primarily, if not entirely, through the resources programmed within each human being.

In 1977, when Valere was diagnosed as having breast cancer, some people wanted to know why we didn't use relaxation and the rest to heal it. We did, but we also got the best medical care we could find. In opting for a lumpectomy and radiation, we were not turning our backs on our own healing convictions. We have always believed in and advocated getting the best that works in any field. Our choice of radiation therapy instead of a mastectomy, detailed in our book, *You CAN Save Your Breast* (W.W. Norton, 1982), both scandalized our surgeons and disappointed our friends who wanted to see us do it without medical science. Our choice of Dr. Luther W. Brady, an eminent radiologist and head of that department at Hahnemann Hospital in

Philadelphia, was an inspired one, we believe—the answer to a lot of prayer and meditation. We believe Dr. Brady and his sophisticated program of radiology saved both Valere's breast and her life. Both Valere's experience and mounting statistical data have indicated that we made the right choice for us.

But this doesn't mean Valere was merely a passive recipient. From the beginning to the end of the therapy, Valere was mentally, emotionally, and spiritually an active participant with faith in God, trust in her physician and his therapy, and utilizing every technique and discipline that might possibly participate in bringing about a happy conclusion to her case. While receiving the radiation for five weeks as an outpatient, she prepared for each brief encounter with the radiation machine by using relaxation, meditation, and visualization. "I calmly visualized the rays going precisely where they were supposed to go and nowhere else. I visualized the rays overcoming the cancer cells and then, later, when I urinated, I visualized the dead cells being expelled from my body." Valere also used visualization in a futuristic way: "I would see myself years hence, standing before a large audience, appearing in the best of health, and saying, "Twenty-five years ago I had breast cancer. Because I chose radiation instead of a mastectomy, I guess some people thought of me as a foolhardy rebel, but here I am a quarter of a century later with both my breast and my life."

Radiation therapy enabled Valere's body to heal itself of breast cancer and Valere's own positive participation in the healing process helped her body to do what it could do. But there are a lot of people who do not respond to the best of therapies, even when they have a good prognosis for recovery.

We believe there are two common errors today in people's response to the role of the person in healing. The first of these is to reject it or minimize its importance. The second is to focus on it to the exclusion of everything else. Disease is always the result of a complex of factors: hereditary predispositions, health habits, exposure to disease agents (germs, carcinogens, etc.), previous health history, environment, and the personality set. Not one of these causes us to become ill, although all can contribute toward that state. Some people have hereditary predispositions to certain diseases, but do not become ill with them. Others are exposed to harmful disease agents and do not become ill. Others remain well despite poor health habits or an unhealthy environment and some Type A personalities do not become coronary victims. Neither sickness nor recovery are quite that simple.

If some people are guilty of oversimplification on the physical side of disease, others are equally naive in oversimplifying the role of the psyche. Some get so carried away in preaching personal responsibility for, and participation in, sickness and health, they make others feel guilty if they are unable to be healed. The mind/body approach is not a magic wand that can cure every disease and save every patient. In fact, all of us need to be reminded of our human mortality: our bodies are not created to last forever. Eventually, we all die of something, whether piecemeal or all at once like the wonderful "One Horse Shay." Furthermore, as Achterberg and Lawlis remind us, "For every disease there appears to be a point of no return. . . . To accuse these patients of not wanting to get well is inappropriate . . . The effort required may be beyond their capacity to respond."[1]

More of the people we meet, however, seem to err on the side of expecting too little from the body/mind approach. Our criticism of many medical professionals is that they too often discount it and set the patient's "point of no return" too early just because they have exhausted all medical, but not personal, resources.

So, acknowledging the limitations of the body/mind concept and the excesses of some of its advocates, we will spend the

---

[1]Jeanne Achterberg and G. Frank Lawlis, *Bridges of the BodyMind* (Champaign, IL: Institute for Personality and Ability Testing, 1980), p. 10

rest of this chapter outlining its amazing, and for the most part unutilized potentials. For, if some people make too much of it, most people, we have found, make too little of it.

If you are interested in using some of these concepts to either maintain your health or improve it, first you need to be absolutely honest with yourself: is health and wholeness what you really want? If you are ill, do you really want to be healed? "Of course, I do," you say, "otherwise why would I be reading this chapter?" But we've already demonstrated elsewhere in this book that what you say and even what you think may not be what you really want deep down inside where those matters are really decided.

Because they have never found anything positive to live for, some people unconsciously hold on to disease because it's all they have; it's the familiar, if painful, glue that holds them together. We often say that for some people illness is a way of life. "Not me!" you retort. Well, just for a moment, take a good look inside to make sure that illness is not your way of life.

Illness is a way of life when it serves as the organizing focus of your daily life; when it occupies the largest part of your thinking; or when it becomes the way in which you identify yourself. Who am I? — a patient, a sick person, a diabetic, a cardiac, and so forth. Illness is also a way of life when it becomes a means to an end — to control, to escape, to cope, to punish, to get attention, to get love, etc. Illness is a way of life when it manifests a dislike or disregard for your own body; when it represents the polarization of your capacity for concern and care. You cannot be concerned for others when you are the center of a universe which revolves around you and your malady. Illness is a way of life when it becomes the basis for your religion and defines your relationship to God. ("My religion is based on trying to get Divine aid for ME." Beyond that, God serves no other purpose.) Your illness or incapacitation could also become the source of a kind of perverted pride. Some people are proud of their diseases for they represent battle scars — their "purple hearts."

We have never met anyone who would say "yes" to all these symptoms, but we have known people who in rare candor could say "yes" to some of them. Emotions can have an adverse reaction upon the body. One of those adverse reactions is a lowered level of resistance against disease agents. This is no longer a matter of conjecture. There are scads of data we can cite. Previously we cited data indicating that poor adjustment to stress factors can result in a shrinkage (or atrophy) of the lymph nodes—an important part of the body's defense system. We also mentioned that stress may result in a disappearance of white blood cells—another vital factor in the defense complex. Some of the harmful effects which stress may introduce into our bodies are tissue damage or an overproduction of hormones that in excessive amounts attack the body. Adrenal corticoids are part of the body's defense system: they promote inflammation in the body so that poisons can be isolated. But when there is an overproduction of corticoids, they are likely to raise blood pressure to dangerous levels, and can cause kidney disease or tears in the walls of our arteries. It has also been demonstrated that distress raises the level of sugar in the bloodstream, even for non-diabetics.

These harmful effects are not limited to grand emotions and dramatic personality disorders. Neurochemist Jack Barchas of Stanford says that even subtle behavior can influence biochemistry. In fact, available data seems to indicate that every thought affects the body in some way. Even when the effect of an experience may not seem all that dramatic, it may be enough to create an imbalance in body chemistry.

Wholeness is not so much a matter of the presence or absence of something in the body, but of the delicate balance of that which is present. This balance is called *homeostasis*; disease may be the end result of an absence of it and healing the consequence of the re-establishment of it. We need adrenalin, but too much will cause us harm. We need cholesterol to plug up the tears in the arteries, but too much of it—and particularly of the wrong kind—can seriously harm us by clogging up those vessels. So, it is the disturbance of the *homeostatic* balance that makes us vulnerable to the germs that ordinarily we fight off, to carcinogens that normally do not affect us, and to predispositions that are otherwise not manifested in our health. This is what Dr. Claude Bernard called "the terrain" — the receptivity of the human body to disease agents. It is reported that, although Bernard and Pasteur disagreed on this concept, on his deathbed, Pasteur reportedly exclaimed, "Bernard was right, the microbe is nothing, the terrain everything."[2]

A large part, although not the whole, of the terrain is emotional health. This is manifested not only in our emotional states, but also in our personality profiles and lifestyles. In fact, it is held that most of the ten top diseases suffered in the USA today are lifestyle diseases, as Achterberg and Lawlis put it, "the result of things that we do to ourselves, or things that we expose ourselves to without proper defense."[3]

Approaching this from a different perspective, we can also say that emotions, personality factors, and even lifestyles can be the key to our recovery, because these factors can be changed by new ways of thinking and acting, even under the old circumstances. The most important factor in healing, therefore, is the notion of recovery. If that is not present, it is very difficult for it to occur. Sigmund Freud recognized this: "Expectation colored by hope and faith is an effective force with which we have to reckon in *all* our attempts at treatment and cure."[4]

In their excellent book, *Bridges of the BodyMind,* Achterberg and Lawlis recount their research into the use of imagery with patients suffering from various diseases, including cancer, diabetes mellitus, chronic back pain, rheumatoid arthritis, alcoholism and severe burns. They asked patients to draw their

---

[2]Jeanne Achterberg, *Imagery in Healing* (Boston: New Science Library) 1985, p. 162.
[3]Achterberg and Lawlis *Bridges of the BodyMind*, p. 2.
[4]Achterberg and Lawlis, *Bridges of the BodyMind,* p. 37.

mental images of (1) the disease or disorder, (2) the treatment, and (3) the personal defense or ability to fight disease. If, for example, the patient drew his disease as a large monster, dwarfing everything else, it indicated to the researchers that the unconscious attitude toward the disease was likely to inhibit the body from fighting it and overcoming it. The same conclusion could be drawn when the treatment was depicted as puny as compared to the disease. These images pretty much indicated which patients would interact successfully with their therapy. It also pretty well indicated those who would not be helped by a program of treatment. Sometimes the researchers were successful in getting patients to change their mental images of one or more of the three factors. And sometimes the changes in imagery were accompanied by improvement and recovery.

Mental images, we must remember, exert tremendous control over the body—for good or ill. When we are in control of these mental images, even when we don't consciously "see" them as pictures, we can gain a significant degree of control over our bodies for self-regulation. This is true when effecting healing as well as in preventing illness.

In the Hartley Films production of *Biofeedback: The Yoga of the West*, there is a sequence in which Dr. Elmer Green is seen testing Jack Schwartz, a remarkable American yogi. In this sequence, Schwartz is demonstrating his yogic control over his body by pushing large unsterilized knitting needles through his arm, apparently without any sensation of pain, with perfect control of bleeding, and without regard for possible infection. Green tells us that, when asked how he prevented infections, Schwartz said that if the body understands that it is not to interact with or react to any foreign material, there is no way that an infection can start.

Unless you have that kind of control over your body (and if you do, why are you reading this book?), we do not recommend you try to duplicate any part of Schwartz's feat. Nor would we want to try an equally amazing display of control over the human body: Sri Lankans walking slowly and blithely over long, hot coal beds without feeling any pain or injury. Nevertheless, these and many other examples give us some clue to the possibilities of self-regulation, particularly in some of the less dramatic and colorful areas of human experience.

So many people go through life full of fears—of foods, drafts, germs, getting wet, being too dry, and so on. Instead of merely cataloging all the things to which we seem to be super-sensitive or vulnerable, wouldn't it be worthwhile to spend as much time teaching your mind/body not to react to some of these agents? Is it not likely that much of your sensitivity or vulnerability to these agents is caused by fear, by focusing attention upon them?

In chapter 2 we discussed the symbolism of the half-empty or half-full glass. It is the focus of your attention that plays such a large role in your experience of pain. The degree of pain you experience is in proportion to the amount of attention you give it. Focus on your pain and it is likely to continue longer and stronger. Focus away from your pain and its effect will be less. At Dr. Norman Shealy's pain clinics patients are not allowed to talk about their pains except at scheduled times with therapists. This is not because pain isn't real or because the staff is unsympathetic, but because they have found that continually verbalizing pain focuses attention on it and thereby increases your perception of it. The best way to handle pain, apart from medications, is not to deny it or try to act like it isn't there, but to focus your attention on something else.

HOW CAN YOU LEARN TO USE YOUR INNER POWER OF SELF-HEALING?

Redundant as it may seem to say so, you can use relaxation and meditation to prepare yourself for healing. We teach relaxation to anyone who comes to us with a physical problem because relaxation is the best preparation to healing. Relaxation helps release your inner power of self-healing. A relaxed state will also help you get the most out of your medical therapy. Meditation is also helpful and some physicians recommend meditation as a part of their therapeutic program. Robert Keith Wallace's Ph.D. research at UCLA demonstrated the effectiveness of meditation in influencing the basal metabolism rate.[5]

You can also utilize the healing power of dreams. We made some references to this in chapter 8, although the emphasis there was on essentially emotional healing. Dreams can also be very helpful in physical healing and this is an old concept. In ancient Greece, the cult of Aesclepius made extensive use of dreams to elicit physical healing. We have visited the shrines of Aesclepius at Kos, Epidaurus, and Pergamon. At the latter, you can still see the Sacred Tunnel, where sleep incubation was practiced. Following a three-day fast, patients would sleep in the temple precincts, while priests suggested dreams in which Aesclepius would appear with a serpent entwined on his staff. These dreams were often instrumental in effecting a cure.

Using the techniques outlined in chapter 8, you may program your dreams and ask your unconscious to tell you the cause of your illness, the barriers to healing, and what therapies might be followed. You might also program your dreams for an encounter with the Great Physician — Christ, the Divine Light, or your own Inner Physician.

In order for dream therapy to work, you need to develop a positive attitude and reinforce it with imagery. We realize this may seem to be redundant advice, but it's hard to overemphasize either of these concepts. We hope we have made a case for both the healing power of the positive and the unhealthy power of the negative. Today we received a letter from friends in New Mexico. Enclosed was a Chuck Vadun

---

[5]Walter McQuade and Ann Aikman, *Stress — What it is, What It Can Do to Your Health, How to Fight Back*, (New York: E.P. Dutton, 1974) p. 183.

cartoon, showing a patient in a hospital bed with a physician standing over him saying, "Our tests show you're allergic to your own negative thoughts." Search for those cognitive distortions that give rise to poor self-esteem and depression, so you can root out the negative thoughts that may be harmful to your physical health. These would include negative attitudes about your body, the inevitability of illness or suffering, your fate as a lifelong patient, your body as weak and impotent, or your ailments as permanent, pervasive conditions.

Changing negative thoughts can be effected with programs of mental imagery. When possible, demonstrate your powers of self-healing on some relatively minor ailment. This will give you the confidence to be more effective when things are more serious. (Of course, we realize you may not have this option.) With children we have often demonstrated the inner power of healing by telling them to rid themselves of a wart through "telling it to go away." Children are very effective at this because they are much less cynical than adults.

If headaches are an occasional or frequent problem, this might be a good project to begin to learn self-healing techniques. Tension headaches are particularly amenable to self-healing. Migraines also may be manageable or curable, particularly with the use of biofeedback training. Relaxation and imagery are very effective.

Of course, not all headaches are triggered by stress and emotional states. You may be predisposed to headaches by heredity. Triggers to headaches are some physical activities, hormones, specific foods, personal circumstances, posture, noise, poor light, and so forth. Among the foods that may trigger headaches are those that contain *tryamine* (dairy products, citrus foods, bananas, pineapples, organ meats, fermented or pickled foods, onions, nuts, broad beans, or red wines), *monosodium glutamate,* processed meats with nitrite compounds (hot dogs, bologna, bacon), caffeine (coffee, tea, cola, Anacin, Excedrin), and alcoholic beverages. It would be well to monitor your intake of the above foods while working with relaxation and other self-healing methods.

GUIDED HEALING MEDITATIONS

If your headaches or other physical problems are attributable in whole or in part to stress and emotional states, meditation is often one of the most effective means of tapping into your own considerable powers of self-healing. Although a few people may find immediate help from their very first try at such a meditation, usually results follow persistent practice of these procedures. Lots of medical prescriptions and therapies are not immediately effective either. If you use any of the following healing meditations, we suggest that you first record them on a tape cassette so that you can devote more energy and attention to the meditation process.

The Great Physician

After you have achieved a relaxed, passive state of mind, envision yourself in a beautiful green meadow. Hear the songs of birds, smell the flowers, feel the breeze, and taste a blade of grass. When you feel very comfortable in the meadow, look across it and see a group of people surrounding a tall figure in white. Walk toward that group. As you walk toward them, you recognize that the tall figure in white is the Healing Christ. As you walk toward him, you see him place his hands upon people to heal them. A deaf man receives back his power of hearing. A lame woman is healed and walks away. The demons of drug abuse are exorcised from a youth. A word, the touch of his hands, and the people go away giving thanks for being made whole.

Now you stand before him and look up into his face. His face is one of both strength and compassion. As he looks into your eyes there is unconditional love and you feel that love enter your body, mind and spirit, until you, too, are whole. Having received his healing touch, you remember one or more others who need it, and you bring them to stand with you as he lays his hands upon them.

At last, you turn from him and walk back across the meadow, knowing that his healing love goes with you, even as you return to your normal state of consciousness. As you count to three to open your eyes, you know that you will return renewed, refreshed, healed and full of vitality.

The Healing Light

After you have achieved a relaxed, passively alert state of mind, you see yourself floating on your back on a fluffy white cloud in a beautiful blue sky. You are completely relaxed, completely at peace. For this moment, you have left all concerns and troubles behind you in that other world of things and materiality. The world you are in now is the eternal, the real world of spirit. In this world you are home at last. You feel the coolness of the breeze and the gentle warmth of the sun. The only sound is the gentle breeze that sometimes passes over you. The air is fresh and clean and it seems you can smell the very purity of it.

As you continue to float peacefully and effortlessly through the sky, you see a beam of golden light reaching down from the highest heavens. It is a warm and gentle golden light of healing. The beam first comes to rest on your forehead at the area sometimes called the third eye. Here it enters your body, gently encompassing the upper part of your head, gently expanding down into your face and throat, continuing on down your shoulders into your arms, hands and fingers; moving down gently over your chest—heart, lungs, alimentary canal—to your stomach, intestines, bowels and genitals; down over your back, down your spine, over the small of your back, down over your buttocks, through your upper and lower legs, down through your ankles and into your feet and toes.

Having filled your body with this golden healing light, it continues to grow and expand within you, filling every organ, every tissue, every nerve, every cell — until your whole body is permeated with the healing light that grows and grows and grows. If there is some place or places in the body that need special attention, by the very direction of your thought you can send an additional volume of the light to that part or parts.

The healing light continues to grow and expand within you until at last it spills forth from you and fills the room where you are, the whole house or building, flowing out into the community, the nation, and the world. Wherever there are those in special need, you can — by the power of your thought — especially direct the light to them. Wherever there are places of tension, strife, tyranny, and suffering, you can direct the light.

At last, knowing that the light has made you one with God or the cosmos, and has linked you to all other creatures everywhere, you prepare to return to your normal state of consciousness. Your cloud, like a leaf, slowly circles downward until you come to rest upon the earth once more. But the healing light still lives wtihin you and still makes you one with all life.

RESOURCES FOR FURTHER STUDY AND SELF-DEVELOPMENT

Althouse, Lawrence W. *Rediscovering the Gift of Healing.* York Beach, ME: Samuel Weiser with Spiritual Frontiers Fellowship, 1983.

Althouse, Larry & Valere. *You Can Save Your Breast.* New York: W.W. Norton, 1982, Chapters 9, 10.

Benson, Herbert, M.D. *The Mind/Body Effect.* New York: Simon & Schuster, 1979.

———. *Beyond the Relaxation Response.* New York: New York Times Books, 1984.

Borysenko, Joan. *Minding the Body, Mending the Mind.* Reading, MA: Addison-Wesley, 1987.

Cousins, Norman. *Anatomy Of An Illness.* New York: W.W. Norton, 1979.

———. *The Healing Heart.* New York: W.W. Norton, 1983.

Dossey, Larry, M.D. *Space, Time & Medicine.* Boston: New Science Library, 1982.

———. *Beyond Illness.* Boston: New Science Library, 1984.

Leshan, Lawrence. *You Can Fight For Your Life.* New York: M. Evans, 1977.

McMillen, S.I., M.D. *None of These Diseases.* Old Tappan, NJ: Spire, 1963.

Ornstein, Robert & Sobel, David. *The Healing Brain.* New York: Simon & Schuster, 1987.

Oyle, Dr. Irving. *The Healing Mind.* Milbrae, CA: Celestial Arts, 1975.

Ryan, Regina Sara and Travis, John W., M.D. *Wellness Workbook.* Berkeley, CA: Ten Speed, 1981.

Shealy, C. Norman, M.D. *The Pain Game.* Millbrae, CA: Celestial Arts, 1976.

———. *90 Days to Self-Health.* New York: Dial Press, 1977.

Siegel, Bernie S. *Love, Medicine & Miracles.* New York: Harper & Row, 1986.

Simonton, O. Carl, M.D., Stephanie Matthews-Simonton, James Creighton. *Getting Well Again.* Los Angeles: J.P. Tarcher, 1978.

Steadman, Alice. *Who's the Matter With Me?* Marina del Rey, CA: DeVorss, 1977.

Weil, Andrew. *Health & Healing.* Boston: Houghton Mifflin, 1983.

Hartley Foundation Films

Biofeedback: The Yoga of the West (40 minutes)
Body, Mind and Spirit (40 minutes)
Healing and Wholeness: Holistic Health In Practice (35 mintues)
Holistic Health: The New Medicine (35 minutes)

Hypertension: The Mind/Body Connection (28 minutes)
The Therapeutic Touch: Healing in the New Age (35 minutes)

The Hartley Film Foundation
Cat Rock Road
Cos Cob, CT 06807

CHAPTER

WHO'S PUSHING
YOUR
BUTTONS?

If you are married to an alcoholic, if you are the parent of a problem child or the child of domineering parents, if you are a hen-pecked husband or an abused wife, you are likely allowing someone else to press the buttons that control your life—both without and within. Questions like, "How are you?" "Is it a good day for you?" or "How are things going?" are not answered easily because you have to decide whether to tell or hide the truth. Your answer is dependent upon another person. If your husband came home from work tonight sober, then you say, "I'm fine, thank you." If your child actually got to school and the principal's office didn't have to call again, then, "It's been a good day." If you wife hasn't thrown one of her temper tantrums this evening, then you can say, "It's going well with me." If you let someone else influence you to this degree, you cannot be in charge of your life. Call it what you like—not "pulling your own strings," letting others manipulate you, surrendering your autonomy — you are permitting someone else to run what God put into your hands alone — your life, your self.

There are two ways this can manifest. Some people are dominated by the strength of someone else. If you have poor self-esteem, difficulty in asserting yourself, if you are doubtful, fearful or easily put down, you can be the natural prey of those who, instead of devoting themselves to running their own lives, get their kicks by dominating others. You may be afraid because of someone else's physical prowess, size, position, status, a loud and authoritative voice, or a bullying manner.

At the other end of the spectrum are those who are dominated by the weaknesses of others. If you are perceived as strong, you may be easy prey for people who are able to persuade you that you must be strong for them, too. You continually say "yes," when you really want to say "no," but you are afraid if you say "no," the other person's weakness will bring on a tragedy for which you would feel responsible.

What begins as a comfortable dependency-type relationship can turn into a prison from which there seems to be no escape. You no longer feel good about what the other person wheedles out of you, but you are afraid of the consequences if you behave like any other rational human being. You can't stand being in this relationship but you don't know how to get out. Faced with this impasse, some people unwittingly become "passive suicides" — not consciously killing themselves, but losing the will to live, they find a socially acceptable way to die.

How do we get locked into these unhealthy relationships? There are quite a few possible answers. We have found that some people have a distorted idea of love. If you believe that love means you do everything you can for the other person, you may try to make it as easy for that other person as you can. Many people whom we have counseled assumed that by letting someone dominate and even terrorize their lives, they were fulfilling the ideal of Christian love. "Didn't Jesus wash his disciples feet?" The difference is that Jesus gave himself for others, but he was never manipulated by anyone. Although he stooped to wash his disciples feet, his servanthood retained a sovereignty. They did not respect him less for what he did, but more. The Lord, girded with a cloth to wash his disciples' feet, is still the Lord.

People who manipulate you, who push the buttons that set you in motion, do not respect you. In fact, each time they win — either through strength or weakness — they respect you even less. Nor can they love you, except as a thing that exists for their own gratification.

Although it is often represented in a wishy-washy manner, the love practiced and preached by Jesus was not weak — but strong. If it had been weak, Jesus would have told the rich young ruler that, although he really should give away his material possessions, it would be okay if he didn't. In the Judeo-Christian scriptures, love brings out the best in others, not the worst. (We have concentrated on the Christian concept of love here because that is our common background. We suspect that in other religions the concept of love can also be distorted by the practitioners.)

Let's think about love for a moment. If you are someone whose love is frequently stepped on and taken advantage of, is it possible that being a victim rewards you, makes you feel better? We have observed some people start that kind of relationship because it makes them feel good — strong, admirable, in a position of strength. It is wonderful to feel needed by others, but you must be careful that you don't get hooked on just that feeling. It is seductively flattering to always be the strong one, the one who apologizes and forgives (regardless of who's to blame), always giving but not receiving, the savior of those who are not so strong. You can also get satisfaction from being a martyr — the long-suffering saint who is always available to bail someone out (literally or figuratively), to give someone "one more chance," hoping your help may put him or her on the right path.

In the beginning, you may really enjoy the honor and prestige of being Atlas, holding the world on your shoulders.

After a while, however, you may find that you might be better off to pass up the honor. But once you've got the world on your shoulders, the only way to get rid of it is to get someone else to take it from you. Unfortunately, everyone else declines the honor, and you are stuck, holding, not the bag, but the world, and you want to run to the window and shout: "I'm not going to take it any more!"

Actually, that doesn't do much good. People may stop and listen for a moment, but they soon go on their way. There is only one way to get rid of the burden of holding up the world: just put it down — you never had to hold it up anyway! If you are a religious person, you can hand it back to God, although, to be honest, you can't really give it to God because you never had it on your shoulders in the first place. You only thought you did.

We previously warned you against trying to play God. We have just discussed the futility of trying to hold the world on your shoulders. And now we will put it even more plainly: concentrate on taking charge of your own life and let others be in charge of theirs. "Ah, I'd love to," you protest, "but they can't handle it without me. I've seen them fail too often by themselves."

Undoubtedly. And one reason they can't handle it by themselves is that you have taught them that they cannot. Whether or not you did it for the most altruistic reasons, by constantly trying to be responsible for other people you make them dependent upon you. You have also destroyed their self-confidence. In hundreds of ways you've communicated to them that what they need is not what they have. To get by — to keep a job, to stay in school, to keep out of jail, or whatever — you've told them they need you. Whatever you got out of the relationship in its early stages has now turned bittersweet for both of you. Instead of love, what you have at best is love/hate and at worst, a barely tolerant contempt.

The real tragedy of this type of relationship is that, although you think you are fulfilling the requirements of love, you are not really doing the loving thing for the other person by allowing him or her to go through life as a manipulator. Your "love" does not bring out the best in the other person, even though it seems that "just one more time" might do the trick and turn around the person's descent into Hell.

Some years ago, Larry counseled a woman married to a very prominent industrialist and political personality. What most people did not know, Larry learned, was that the man was an alcoholic whose life was barely held together by the slavish devotion of his wife, as well as the fearful efforts of his family and closest staff members.

"I can't stand one more day of this," she told Larry. The husband made hundreds of promises to get help, but reneged on every one. Members of the family pleaded with him, threatened him, and appealed to every motivation they knew, but nothing worked. Life in the family and his office was a living hell. When he was sober, it was "a good day" for everyone. When he was drunk, everyone was miserable. When he was hungover, everyone tiptoed around the house and office, speaking in whispers so as not to disturb the "monster."

The woman was suffering from a number of physical complaints, in fact, that was what had originally brought her to Larry. It soon became apparent, however, that these physical problems were the consequence of the stress that she had to endure daily. "Well, if you can't stand one more day of this," said Larry, "I suppose you've considered leaving him?"

"Yes," she replied, "I don't know what else to do; I've tried everything else."

"Your leaving him might be the one thing that will motivate him to get some help," Larry offered.

Not long after she did leave and Larry didn't hear from her for quite a while. Then, one day, he encountered her, and from the look on her face, he knew that she had gone back to her husband.

"It sounds strange, I suppose," she explained, "but for twenty-five years I've done nothing else than be the wife of an alcoholic. When I left him, I found I had nothing to do, nothing to live for." She found she needed his alcoholism as much as he did.

Of course, neither of these people really "needed" alcoholism, but they both decided that they wanted it for whatever meaning it gave to their lives. If that strikes you as a pretty sick relationship, then let us point out that there are multitudes of "sick" relationships which people consciously or unconsciously choose, rather than risk a mature, healthy one that requires work and effort instead of complaining.

We're not saying that people don't have the right to choose that kind of relationship, if that's what they want. But don't spend the rest of your life complaining about it, unless that's what you really want from life — the justification to go through life complaining and seeking sympathy.

In a previous chapter we told you that, early in his life, Larry rather enjoyed sympathy. "For a while," he says, "it was an interesting role. "Nobody Knows The Trouble I've Seen" was my theme song — although through my self-dramatization they could hardly not know the trouble I'd seen, or imagined. But, eventually, somewhere along the way I decided that my cup of sympathy had pretty well been filled and was running over. Now I wanted something else."

Larry also discovered as a young pastor what all of us need to understand: You cannot do for someone else what they will not do for themselves. You cannot force someone to be well who wants to be sick. As he found with several of his parishioners, you cannot keep them alive if they want to die. You can stand ready to help and offer a hand when they shoulder their burden, but you cannot bear the burden for them. Only one person has ever been able to do that and much of our trouble stems from the fact that we forget that we are not God.

It is enough to take charge of your own life. And we can really only help other people when somehow they are enabled to do that too. That is the truly loving thing we can do. One organization calls this "Tough Love." We agree, for weak love is not love at all. It is just weakness.

It is important to distinguish between doing the loving thing and feeling love. Since the 1960s, love has become really "in" — "What the World Needs Now Is Love," "Love Makes The World Go Round," "Make Love Not War," and so on. The sentiment is certainly noble, but the reality is not much of an improvement, if any, on whatever we thought about love before. Coupled with the admonition, "If it feels good, do it," there is a popular impression that love is essentially a feeling. So a lot of people abstain from doing loving things because they don't have loving feelings.

This may be harmful for two reasons. On one hand, if we feel "loving," we may be led to do something simply for the purpose of sustaining that feeling. That may make us feel "good," but it may not really be good for the other person. The other danger, of course, is that we may hold back on loving acts because there is an absence of loving feelings. We need to do the loving thing, whether or not we feel loving. Ironically, often it is only after we have done the loving thing that we find ourselves able to feel loving. Acts are dependent upon attitudes and feelings usually follow acts.

So what does this have to do with having your buttons pushed? Many people misunderstand love; instead they set up unrealistic expectations of their own roles, and become very susceptible to manipulation by others.

We have been discussing being in charge of yourself. You should not control others, nor should you let others control you. This means you need to learn control so that other people cannot manipulate you. And if you are in charge of yourself, you cannot permit yourself to be ruled by your own autonomous emotions either.

Because it is the one emotion that often troubles people most, we will focus momentarily upon anger. Lots of people are under the domination of their own anger. They don't want to lose control, but the anger seems to be stronger than they are. When someone or something presses their "anger button," they feel like helpless victims of their own emotional machinery.

Perhaps it would be helpful if you understood that the "anger button" is part of your human endowment, placed there for the purpose of self-preservation. Fear and anger are closely linked because they both are concerned with self-preservation. Anger, therefore, like fear, is neither inherently bad or good. The key, as with so many things in human nature, is what you do with it.

Some of your problems with anger may be that you have been led to believe that all anger is bad. Nice people, it is assumed, do not get angry. Christians should not get angry—leaving some of you rather uncomfortable with those occasional reports of Jesus' anger. The end result for many of you is either a terrible fear of your anger or a denial of it—which sometimes leads to acting it out in thinly disguised behavior.

We all know what some people do with anger—they find people and things upon which to vent it—sometimes us! But there are others, just as angry, who react by withdrawing, especially if they feel guilty about their anger. Many people learn anger habits which are no less harmful because they attempt to conceal it—the husband or wife who doesn't talk for two days and then when asked, "Are you angry?" says, "Who, me?"

Most anger-coping behavior is injurious to yourself and others. Let's assume you have a dispute with your partner and leave the house with it unresolved. Have you really coped with your anger by clenching your teeth, constricting your breathing, raising your blood pressure, producing noradrenalin which your body doesn't know what to do with, and getting heartburn? Or are you any more successful with your anger if you vent it on "safe targets"—store clerks, waiters, children, or subordinates?

One of the worst features about this kind of anger control is that it allows you to think you handled the anger simply because you avoided a full-scale confrontation. When you stifle anger and sweep it under the carpet, you end up attacking yourself. It's like a driver with one foot on the accelerator and the other on the brake. When you are bottled up like this, you cannot be very creative; you cannot show love; and you don't solve your problem.

The physical toll can be considerable. Dr. Kenneth Pelletier says, "There is considerable evidence that internalized anger induces prolonged stress reactivity, which is more damaging than the transient strain involved in the immediate expression of anger."[1] So, concealment and repression of anger can be a major factor in psychosomatic illness, as well as in cancer and arthritis. To compensate for this, a lot of people think the solution to burying anger must be to let it explode all over the place whenever they feel it coming on! This is likely to cause as many problems as it may seem to solve. What then can we do with our anger?

First, as we have already suggested, you need to acknowledge and accept your anger, instead of denying it and sweeping it under the carpet. That means that you will make an attempt to deal with it.

Second, you will need to try to understand what your anger is and why you become angry in certain situations. An old African hunter once said that he had learned very early in his career that when you go out hunting ivory, you invariably discover that "there's an elephant attached!" When you investigate and probe your experience of anger, you will probably find other factors attached. For example, what you experience as anger may really be your way of expressing frustration. You feel powerless to do what you want to do and become angry — usually with yourself and your own impotence, even if you blame someone or something else. Anger may also be an

---

[1]Kenneth Pelletier, *Mind as Healer — Mind as Slayer* (New York: Dell, 1977), p. 106.

expression of fear. As long as *homo sapiens* have inhabited this planet, anger has been used to meet the challenge of something frightening. The threat to you may be physical or emotional, but you nevertheless become angry in order to meet that threat. Anger may also be your reaction to anything that seems to threaten your self-esteem and you become angry so that you may defend it from shame, ridicule, or embarrassment.

So the next time you experience anger—expressed or unexpressed—try to analyze why you are reacting that way. You are likely to say that someone or something "makes you mad," but the real source of your anger is likely to be something within you, not something external. The external—the chair that gets in your way, your neighbor's dog, a friend's remark that you find insulting—is only the occasion for your anger. So the key to your anger, then, is often to be found, not in something outside you, but the way you see, interpret and react to some external event. Since you seldom can change the externals, your best strategy is to change the way you perceive and react to your perceptions. Just as Dr. David Burns believes most depression is a thinking or cognitive disorder—we feel depressed because we have been thinking somewhat irrationally—so anger may often be the result of distorted cognitions. Our feeling buttons are pushed by our distorted thoughts—our misperceptions of what we think other people feel and intend toward us, the unrealistic values we place on certain events, and our exaggeration of the consequences. The behavior that seemed a calculated affront—is that really what the other person meant to convey? Does it really matter if someone shoved into line ahead of you—is your honor really so wounded as to make it worthwhile calling in the fight-or-flight response in your body and getting up a full head of steam with nowhere to go and nothing to do? Just as examining your thoughts, perceptions and attitudes can help you dispel depression, so, if you work at it, can you pull the plug on anger.

There are two constructive alternatives to burying anger or exploding on others. The first is to learn how to express anger in a way that is not destructive. Learn to express it early enough—before your feelings have become distorted by pressure. This may mean telling someone that something annoys you, instead of waiting until the annoyance has turned into a federal case. Much of the destruction related to anger is caused when anger is denied and repressed. In effect, repressing anger is like putting it in a pressure cooker—when it finally comes out, it's too hot to handle!

The second way to express anger (or pre-anger annoyance and irritability) is to attack behavior not people. Many conflicts get out of hand, not becuase the grievance is not reasonable, but because the other person feels personally attacked and must counterattack in order to insure self-preservation. Instead of saying, "You're no good and you've never been any good," it would be a lot more effective to say, "What you've just done really makes me angry, and it's made me angry before." Problems handling anger are caused by verbal overkill. The other person responds to the intemperate way in which you verbalize your feelings, not your gripe.

It is even better if you can focus on your feelings instead of the other person. So, instead of saying, "You make me angry," you could say, "When you do that, I get very angry." By not putting the other person completely on the defensive, there is the possibility that the confrontation can serve a constructive purpose by clearing the air.

Instead of bottling up (or blowing up), you can learn to defuse your angry feelings. This is not the same as denying them or sublimating them. Rather, it is an attempt to change your reaction to the situation. Your feelings may really not be justified. Actually, sometimes your angry response may be little more than a role that you play for the sake of achieving some purpose—getting your way, working out another emotion, or living up to what you think is expected of you. So you may act angry because you think you ought to be angry. Unfortunately, although this may begin as role playing, you may get so far into your role that you suffer the same consequences. You may throw a temper tantrum to get your way, but your body doesn't know it's an act and it will probably react in a way that is destructive to your physical and emotional well-being. The social damage — how other people react — is no less likely to be harmful either.

So, it is very important to accept, recognize and work with your anger so that you may be fully in control of who or what pushes your buttons.

LEARNING TO PUSH YOUR OWN BUTTONS

So that you may be more aware of who pushes your buttons, make a study of your important relationships. On a piece of paper, write down the names of people with whom you have important relationships. These should include all the relationships that affect your emotional health in some way — family members, friends, neighbors, employees, bosses, subordinates, and so forth. After you have listed all the names, indicate *who* does the button-pushing in each realtionship — you, the other person, or each of you pushing your own. How does this last answer affect the relationship? Make notes. Think about each of the relationships, if any, in which the *other* person is pushing your buttons. Why does this happen? Does it have to be? After you've thought about this, write the following statement in big, bold letters: NO ONE CAN TAKE ADVANTAGE OF ME VERY LONG WITHOUT MY HELP.

In each of the relationships where you indicated you are being taken advantage of, ask yourself how you are helping others manipulate or take advantage of you. Write down what you could do to change the situation, if you wanted to. Finally, ask yourself: do you really want to change the situation? If so, make specific plans on how to go about making the change.

Make a complete complaint analysis so you will be conscious of what pushes your buttons. Make a list of your major complaints that involve relationships. Examples might be: "My husband won't talk to me; my wife always has a headache, the new pastor at church is going to drive everyone away," and so forth. Next to each complaint, list the name(s) of the people with whom you share these complaints. Keeping in mind our earlier statement—IF IT'S WORTH COMPLAINING ABOUT, IT'S WORTH DOING SOMETHING ABOUT IT—consider each complaint and what you might do about it if you wanted to. Write down your answers. Decide which of these you will respond to with action.

You can also make an anger inventory to learn how much anger you have been storing all these years. On a piece of ruled paper, write the following words in the lefthand column, one below the other: WHO?—WHAT?—WHEN?—WHERE?—HOW?—WHY? To the right of each of these headings, write in the appropriate answers to: *These Make Me Angry.* Remembering that distorted cognitions—perceptions and attitudes—can cause you to be unnecessarily angry, search each of these answers to determine what cognitive distortions may play a role in these situations. For example: "when my boss criticizes my work, I assume he's getting ready to fire me," or "when my husband doesn't like what I have prepared for dinner, I tend to feel personally rejected," or "when they didn't vote for me as church trustee, I felt that no one there liked me." Then, ask yourself what would happen if you were to change this idea?

Meditation To Heal Relationships

The following meditation is meant to be used when you have anger, hostility or other negative personal feelings against a particular person. He or she may, or may not, reciprocate your feelings. Concentrate only on your own feelings. First, prepare yourself for meditation with progressive relaxation.

Visualize a religious figure whom you revere—Christ for Christians. In your mind's eye see that figure standing next to the person with whom you're having a problem. See that religious figure place an arm around the shoulders of your problem-person. Know that this gesture is a sign of the figure's love and acceptance of that person. Then, see yourself walk into the picture. The religious figure beckons you to come and join him. You walk toward him and he extends the other arm to you. Now he stands with one arm about you, the other about your problem-person. The straight line formed by the three of you begins to become a triangle, as the religious figure begins to use his outstretched arms to bring the two of you closer. You realize that you cannot be one with the religious figure unless you are also one with the problem-person. At this point, you join arms with him or her. As a result of the closing of this human circuit, you feel a wave of peace and serenity course through the three of you as you stand arm-in-arm. The religious figure assures you that this sense of peace will remain with you when you return to your normal state of consciousness. Count to three and slowly open your eyes.

RESOURCES FOR FURTHER STUDY AND SELF-DEVELOPMENT

Dyer, Dr. Wayne W. *Pulling Your Own Strings.* New York: Thomas Y. Crowell, 1978.

Ellis, Albert, Ph.D. *Anger: How To Live With and Without It.* Secaucus, NJ: Citadel, 1977.

Jampolsky, Gerald G. *Goodbye To Guilt.* New York: Bantam Books, 1985.

Tournier, Paul. *The Violence Within.* New York: Harper & Row, 1978.

Weinberg, Dr. George. *Self Creation.* New York: St. Martin's Press, 1978.

York, Phyllis and David, and Ted Wachtel. *Tough Love.* New York: Doubleday, 1982.

WHEN YOU GET WHERE YOU'RE GOING, WHERE WILL YOU BE?

When you get where you're going, where will you be? We've asked this question of lots of people all over the world. Many people react pretty much the way we did—reflectively and introspectively. However, one man said to us, "I'm not going anywhere; I'm there. In fact," he added, his face clouding over, "I've been there for some time." His words were enigmatic and we did not have the opportunity to pursue the comment with him. Perhaps he was speaking for people who don't think of themselves as going anywhere.

We disagree, of course. Just because it seems that you are standing still doesn't mean you are. Astronomically, whether you leave home or not, the earth is spinning on its axis at tremendous speed. And even as that is happening, the earth is also rotating around the sun, covering millions of miles every year. You may think you're standing still, but you're not!

Of course you knew that—just as you know that from the moment of conception you are moving on a course that carries you through life to death, and, we trust, to something beyond. There may be times when you want to stop the world and get off, but life moves on, even when you think you are standing still.

Life is like Jerome Kern's "Old Man River," who " 'jes keeps rolling along." There may be times when you are "tired of living and skeered of dyin', " but life moves on regardless. Actually, the river is a good analogy for life. The river has a source, and an estuary, and there is a tide that moves all things toward that end. Between the source and the estuary there are ports of call you can choose, you can paddle or row yourself as you wish — sometimes with, sometimes against, the tide. You could also simply drift on this river, and assume, therefore, that you aren't going anywhere. But to drift on the river of life does not keep you from following the tide. Regardless of what you may think, you are never standing still.

So the question is really not whether you are going any-where, but rather: *when you get where you're going, where will you be?* You are going somewhere in life, to be sure, but is it where you intend to go? Is the direction in which you are moving the direction that will take you where you want to go?

Most of us think we have forever to work on that question. But the human "forever" is really a lot shorter than any of us ever imagined. We keep postponing the fullness of life for a "someday" that either never comes or passes us by without our realizing it.

Many people are like Eddie in G. William Jones' modern parable, "Just Around The Corner."[1] As a child, Eddie always believed that the next stage of his life — starting school, going on to high school, graduating — would be the experience that would make life worthwhile. But it never did, for as soon as he would pass on to the next goal, he would find it disappointing

---

[1]G. William Jones, *The Innovator — And Other Modern Parables* (Nashville: Abingdon Press, 1962), pp. 90–92.

and begin to set his sights on the next one: his college diploma, his first job, marrying, getting promotions, having children, buying a bigger home, and finally retirement. Each time he thinks that real living is "just around the corner," and each time he is disappointed. He dies without ever finding the fulfillment that always seemed to be at the next step. When he got where he was going, it wasn't where he really wanted to be.

There are also those who early in life reach some height — real or imagined — and then spend the rest of their lives looking, not ahead to some goal, but always back to that one moment of satisfaction — scoring the winning touchdown in a football game, being chosen valedictorian of their class, or getting the lead in the senior play. One man we knew "came alive" in conversation only when he was recounting his exploits as a bomber pilot in World War II. It was as if nothing of importance had happened since then. He didn't think of himself as going anywhere, because, as he saw it, he had already been there.

Most of us have goals early in life — graduation, college, a job or profession, marriage, children — standard expectations of youth. Ask a young adult where he or she is going and you will probably get some kind of futuristic answer. But what happens? The young adult turns a corner and drops out or moves to new goals — making a million dollars, becoming president of the firm, making the social register, and so forth. And these new goals are either reached or abandoned, and many people settle down to "just living," or drifting with the current.

Although each person moves from birth to death, when you stop setting goals, when you no longer care about achievement, the speed toward the end of life is greatly accelerated. Viktor Frankl, a psychiatrist and proponent of logotherapy, was in a concentration camp during the Second World War. People who were most likely to survive this experience, he found, were those who lived with the expectation of doing something with their lives *after* they survived the camps. Those who drifted with the tide generally did not make it.[2] Achterberg and Lawlis (and many others) have documented that this is no less true with patients in hospitals. Those who have a futuristic outlook — who know what they will do with their health if they regain it — are the ones who respond best to the therapies and are most likely to heal faster and more surely. They are also the ones most likely to survive life-threatening illnesses.

When you have no sense of the future, you are not likely to have much satisfaction in the present. Lots of people we meet are suffering from a disease called *chronic unfulfillment.* The disease is more serious than that name might suggest. It is the worst kind of disease for it is degenerative, painful, crippling, and almost always fatal. It probably kills more people every day than cancer and heart disease together.

In chapter 2 we talked about poor self-esteem, which relates to a failure to feel a sense of achievement. The less you achieve, the less you think of yourself, and the less you think of yourself, the less you attempt. The less you attempt, the less you achieve, and the less experience of success, the more you fear failure. The more you fear failure, the less you risk failure by attempting anything! It's an unending circle.

Of course, if you just want to drift through life, that's your choice. We can't say it's a wrong choice; only "wrong" for us. It may also be true that your life is definitely going where you want it to be going. Again, no one can decide that for you. No one can choose your goals for you or make you achieve them.

Dr. George Ritchie tells of a fascinating experience that happened during World War II. He contracted pneumonia and was pronounced dead. While his body was lying in the morgue, he had what has since come to be called a Near Death Experience (NDE), except that he was near death on the wrong side of the line. Part of his experience included a confrontation

---

[2]Viktor Frankl, *Man's Search for Meaning* (New York: Washington Square), 1963.

with a "Being of Light," whom he identified as the Christ. This Being did not judge him, but, as his life passed in review before him, it was as if he were asking what Ritchie had done with his life. All that Ritchie could think to answer was that he had been an eagle scout. "Somehow," says Ritchie, "that didn't seem to be enough."[3]

That's something that should cause all of us some serious soul-searching: when we've reached our destination and achieved our goals, will it be enough? If the answer is "yes, of course," then perhaps you need read no further. But, if the answer is "no" or even "I'm not sure," then take a few minutes to think about where it is you are headed in life and where it is you would like to reach. Give some thought to and write out answers to the following questions.

What is my life's goal?
Is my current direction going to take me to my goal?
Am I growing, learning, and developing my inner potential, or am I just coasting?
What kind of life would I like to have one year from now?
Five years?
Ten years?
Twenty years?

It is necessary and helpful to look at your life's direction. Whenever you attempt anything in life, it's important to divide complex tasks into smaller, manageable segments. If you focus only on the whole task, you may never get started because it seems so overwhelming. For example, we envisioned this book as a whole, but we wrote it chapter by chapter. And we rewrote some of them along the way—which is what you will do with your life's direction as well.

---

[3]Quoted from the author's notes of an address by Dr. George Ritchie at a Spiritual Frontiers Fellowship Conference, Lake Junnaluska, NC, June 1974.

It is amazing to hear how some people never attempt anything because they are afraid the results will not be good enough. Far better to fail repeatedly than never to try. We all learn by our failures; inactivity teaches nothing, except, perhaps, to do even less. If you are in need of some achievement, you might try the following project:

1) Compile a list of all you do to make life fulfilling and worthwhile. (Examples: I am careful of nutrition; I read worthwhile books to improve my mind, etc.)

2) Now compile a list of behaviors and factors in your lifestyle that might need to be changed or eliminated in order to make your life more in harmony with your lifegoal. (Examples: I am a compulsive eater; I worry too much; I allow myself to feel sorry for myself, etc.)

3) Select one item from the second list to be the focus of a planned-change project. Then list the probable positive effects you will likely experience from making this change. Finally, list the negative effects that will likely occur if you do not. Consider both sets of data, and make a commitment to yourself that you will make this change.

4) Brainstorm how you might go about making this change. (Brainstorming is a process in which you passively allow your mind to suggest as many ideas about a given subject as possible. Write them down — or record them in some way — without judging them as good, bad, impossible, and so forth. Just as the psi flow is usually blocked by a critical attitude toward what you are receiving, so the creative flow reacts much the same way.)

5) Evaluate what you got in the brainstorming session, determining which ideas you can use in your program of planned change. If you don't end up with enough ideas, do the brain-

storming again. The ideas are within your own unconscious; you just have to let them come out. Then, fashion all these ideas into your strategy, writing them down. Included in your strategy may be the following:

- Plan to reward yourself for progress and completion of your project;

- Find support, if available. (For example, if you want to give up smoking, there are a number of support groups you might want to consider.)

- Pick a starting time. You will do better when you make a calendar commitment for beginning and ending a project;

- Provide for record-keeping if it's relevant to your project (like keeping track of weight loss);

- Plan for evaluation (how will you determine your progress in this project?);

6) Evaluate and revise your plan as needed during the project.

You may be saying to yourself at this point, "Yes, I'd like to do something like that *sometime*, the implication being, "But not now!" In the short run it may seem that you don't have enough time. Ironically, you may make that determination because you feel you'll have lots of time in the future. Maybe so. Maybe not.

Several years ago when Valere had breast cancer, she woke up one morning and asked herself, "Am I going to be doing today what I would do if I found I had only a month to live? A week? A day?" That question has made quite a change in the way we view and respond to time. It helped us remember the important distinction in the way the ancient Greeks looked at time. One word, *chronos,* is the way most of us think of time—a succession of seconds, minutes, hours, days, weeks and years — an orderly progression of measured time. The other Greek word for time, however, is *kairos,* which refers, not to the chronological length of time, but the depth of it, or as the Bible speaks of it as "the fullness of time." This is time measured, not in minutes or hours, but in depth and quality. Five minutes spent with one person may be more fulfilling than a half-hour spent with another. So, today we think of life much more in terms of *kairos* than of *chronos.* And we hope to continue to think that way, whether we have another fifty years before us or less.

So, it is not just a matter of whether you see the glass as half-full or half-empty, but how you view and regard your life. You can see it in terms of what is over or what is still before you, of what you lack or what you have, but remember that it is *kairos* that brings you the greatest fullness of time. And focus your attention, indeed your life, not on emptiness, but on fullness. For we have found that when you do, your cup runs over.

ABOUT THE AUTHORS

Larry Althouse is a clergyman and director of the New Dimensions Ministries at First United Methodist Church in Dallas, Texas, where, with Valere, he focuses upon holistic health and human potential development. Valere Althouse was associated for seventeen years with The Green House, a health spa in Arlington, Texas, where she served as a lecturer and consultant. Larry is the author of *Rediscovering the Gift of Healing* (Samuel Weiser, 1982), and together Larry and Valere have written of their experience with breast cancer in *You CAN Save Your Breast* (W.W. Norton, 1982). Larry writes a syndicated newspaper column, "The Bible Speaks," and together they write a weekly travel column, "Travel Talk." Twice a year they take small groups of people to Badgastein, Austria, for their Spa Holiday programs. Larry and Valere combine their experience as counselors and lecturers with a love of travel, and lecture widely in the United States and Europe.